Copy

FOREWARD

Hello, this is my story. It is a true story. I will leave out the names of most of the doctors and hospitals as I am not angry with them. I have a huge distrust for most doctors and there is no place I loathe more than a hospital. The combination of the doctors and hospitals nearly killed me and sent me into a state of mental and physical anguish which I never would have dreamed possible. The following is the story of my journey into deep darkness. More importantly it's the story of how Jesus held me!

Woody Overton

CHAPTER 1

I have always believed in God. I was raised in the Catholic Church by my parents. More so, at the time, by my mother than my father. My father, I believe, went to mass on Sundays to appease my mother. From the beginning, I never doubted what I was being taught. I became an alter boy as soon as I could, following the path of my older brothers. I continued Catholicism until after I was confirmed at the age of 16. When a person completes the Sacrament of Confirmation they are considered an adult in the eyes of the Catholic Church. It is then their responsibility to continue their journey with the Catholic Church.

From that point on I did not chose to follow the rights and rituals of the church except for the occasional Christmas or Easter Mass I attended with my parents or a funeral or wedding that I could not duck out of. Even at these masses I never took communion as I knew my heart was not in it.

I was busy living the life I wanted to live and God was not a concern of mine. I was not an atheist. I still believed in God but he was not foremost in my mind as I lived those years according to my rules.

In 1998, I was working as a correctional officer on a Sunday, on the night shift. I was working at a juvenile detention center and on Sunday nights preachers would come to the detention center to hold non denominational services for any juvenile offenders that wanted to attend.

The juveniles were housed in one man cells with thick iron doors and concrete block walls. They had no interaction with the other juveniles and nothing in their cell other than a mattress, blanket, and a bible. The only time they were out of their cell was to go to or from chow or to shower or the occasional trip to the recreation yard. The juveniles wanted to get out of their cell for any reason that they could and Sunday service was always full.

Let me make mention that these juveniles were incarcerated for serious crimes. Rape, robbery, murder etc. In fact, as my law enforcement career progressed to uniform patrol and then detective I arrested many of these juveniles as they became adults and continued their life of crime.

On this Sunday, a black lady preacher came with some helpers for a service. I had never met her before. Correctional officers escorted the juveniles to the assembly area for the service. I went to the secure area at the front of the prison where the pastor and her helpers were waiting to be escorted through security. I was surprised that the pastor was a female. She appeared to be in her late forties or early fifties, had glasses, was very well dressed and carrying a bible. As I supervised their clearance through security I noticed she was staring at me very intently.

She said to me, " Brother may I speak to you for a minute?"

I answered "Yes." and she waved me over away from the others.

Without introduction she said, "Brother, when I saw you God told me to tell you something."

Now I am thinking, *Okay, here we go –*

She continued and asked me "Do you want to hear what God has to say?"

I said "Yes," thinking to myself, *this ought to be interesting.*

She then told me something that no one on this planet knew, when she finished describing the event she quieted and looked me straight in the eye.

She then said, "God has told me to tell you that what you went through is okay. That what happened to you was horrible but necessary."

She continued to say, "God has not forgotten you and you should not forget or give up on him."

I was blown away. She knew the one thing that happened to me in my life that no one knew or would ever know about because I surely wasn't going to speak of it. I intended to take the secret to my grave. In fact, the incident had happened over 16 years before and I had never told anyone. So here I was meeting this black lady preacher for the first time in my life and she spoke in detail of my deepest secret and that God had told her to tell me he had not forgotten. I was speechless. I didn't know what the emotion was that I was feeling, but I knew it was overwhelming and I knew it came straight from God through the pastors mouth.

She smiled her gentle smile and gave me a motherly hug and said, "God bless you brother."

CHAPTER 2

I did not usually sit in on the Sunday services as I was a supervisor and once the juveniles were secured with the other correctional officers in the service I would leave and go do paperwork. All staff members carried radios and if there was any type of disturbance I would be contacted and would respond accordingly.

Not this Sunday. After listening to what God had to say I was more than intrigued by this pastor. I would have not missed the service for anything.

I went into the service and found out the pastor's name was Shirley Vicks. She was the pastor of the Church of God of Prophecy in Hammond, Louisiana. She began the service with singing songs and to say the least it was a eye opener for me. This was as different from a Catholic Mass as darkness is to light. Pastor Vicks led the service with several more songs that I had never heard before. People were raising their hands and singing. Some were swaying back and forth with their eyes closed. This went on until the music stopped and a quiet hush fell over the crowd.

Pastor Vicks then began to preach and man could she lay the word down. I had never seen anything like it. She preached with conviction. Sometimes loud and sometimes soft but always with authority. She preached about God and Jesus and Satan. She often times would say open your bible to such and such chapter and verse and then quote the scripture that verified what she was preaching. I had never owned a bible and I had never been taught from one. In Catholic mass someone would get up and read a scripture and then the priest would give a sermon. Pastor Vicks service was powerful and moving.

As the service went on I could feel the atmosphere in the room change and it gave me goose bumps. The juveniles and correctional officers were responding to the emotional feelings of the service and it rose to a crescendo to the point at which she asked for any sinners to come forth that wanted to know Jesus.

To my surprise several juveniles and even two correctional officers went forward. She prayed openly with them and asked them to accept Jesus into their lives. People were crying as songs were continuously sung and multiple people went forward and openly accepted Jesus Christ as their savior.

The service concluded and the juveniles were returned to their cells and I made a point to escort Pastor Vicks and her church members out of the facility.

At the front door I asked Pastor Vicks if I could speak with her. She consented. I told her how I was moved beyond words and that I had never witnessed anything like her service and that I knew she was with God. She then invited me to attend her church the next Sunday morning and I agreed without hesitation.

CHAPTER 3

That Sunday came and I arrived at a small red brick church with just a few cars parked in a gravel parking lot. I entered the church into a foyer and then went through a set of swinging double doors and entered the sanctuary. I saw the room was not that large and contained maybe 5 wooden pews on each side. At the front of the room was a raised alter with chairs along the back wall that faced out towards the congregation. The floor was carpeted and the room had numerous windows along the outer walls. The sanctuary was small and bare bones. Nothing fancy- just a simple, plain room.

I observed approximately seven or eight people in the pews and I saw Pastor Vicks at the front of the church. I was just in time for the service to begin as the music had already started. Pastor Vicks looked at me and smiled. Everyone else in the church turned and looked, also. I don't know who was more shocked, me or them. Everyone in the church was black except me. I took a seat at the rear of the sanctuary and began my new life in Christ.

I have never been a racist. I have many great black friends that I have come to know over the years.

I was raised in a small town and went to an all white private school there. Where I was raised the black folks had there side of town and other than seeing blacks at the grocery store or gas station we just didn't interact much.

I joined the Army after graduating high school and served side by side with people of every race. I quickly learned to judge a person on their character and not the color of their skin.

To give you an idea of how segregated our town was but how truly ignorant I was to the segregation I will tell you another true story.

I started working for the Louisiana Department of Corrections when I was 21 years old. My supervisor was a black man named Lieutenant Turner. He was a great guy and taught me a lot about how to conduct myself as a professional. Lieutenant Turner taught me how to interact and deal with inmates. This knowledge served me well throughout my law enforcement career. He took me under his wing and showed me the ropes. I had and still have mad respect for him and the way he handled himself as a professional.

One evening as our shift began I saw Lieutenant Turner did not look well. I asked him what was wrong and he said he was sick and needed to see a doctor, but he did not know of a good one to go to.

I was able to help by suggesting that he see the doctor, in my hometown, that I had been going to my whole life.

I told him about my doctor, how to get there, that my doctor always saw me without an appointment and it never seemed to take long. He was glad to hear it and said he would go first thing in the morning when we got off of our shift.

The next evening after roll call Lieutenant Turner called me to his office. I asked him how his visit to my doctor went.

He said, "Man, I cant believe you did that to me."

I could see he was upset and had no idea why so I asked him what happened.

Lt. Turner told me he arrived at the doctors office and went through the door and sat down in a nice comfortable chair. He said the waiting room was nice and comfortable and had a table which held a large selection of magazines and was very pleasant. He further stated that the floor was carpet and there were nice pictures on the wall.

Then a inner door opened and a nurse asked him if she could help him. He said that he needed to see the doctor and explained his symptoms. Lieutenant Turner further stated that the nurse kind of just looked at him for a minute then told him that he would have to go to the entrance in the back of the building. He said he was confused but he went outside and walked around the building to the back door. When he entered the backdoor he saw a very different waiting room.

He had entered a tiny room which contained a few hard plastic chairs and no magazines, carpet or windows. More importantly the room was packed with people where as the front waiting room only had two patients waiting to see the doctor. The biggest shock was that everyone in this waiting room was black.

I was born and raised in that town and had been going to that doctor's office my entire life. He was an awesome doctor and his head nurse was my best friend's aunt and the mother of a girl I graduated with.

I had been to this office maybe a hundred times and I had not noticed that I had never seen a black person.

I had never really thought about it. I knew the doctor was a great man and I knew his nurse was a awesome christian woman. It just never occurred to me that the office was segregated.

I had never been to the back side of the building where black people had to park and enter the bare bones waiting room. I was shocked and told Lt. Turner so and apologized. He actually started laughing and said that it was okay and he knew I meant no harm.

I include the part about Lt. Turner and the doctor in this book so you can see that while I was not raised as a racist I was raised where I didn't have much personal interaction with black people until I graduated high school and joined the Army.

I loved that doctor and he was dang good at healing and his nurse was one of the sweetest people you will ever meet.

My ignorance of the fact that the office was segregated shows my isolation in growing up in a small town that was largely segregated.

The segregation did not mean the people of the town were bad. It is just the way it was and always had been. It turns out that the doctor saw more black patients than white. Guess what? No black person ever complained about the segregated waiting rooms because they also knew that the doctor was a awesome man and he applied his healing indiscriminately.

Since then the town helped elect the first black District Attorney to ever serve in that parish. Also, now the town has both a black Mayor and Police Chief.

I also should mention that I was the fifth generation of my family to be raised there and that my grandfather on my dads side was the judge there until he died and that my mothers father was the District Attorney there for many years until he retired.

My family never really mentioned race and the only blacks I really interacted with were housekeepers and yard men. One yard man that worked for my parents for well over thirty years until he was murdered in 2012. He was like family and my parents attended his funeral. Our housekeeper still works sometimes for my parents and she is my mothers' dear friend.

The reason I mention my home towns past is to help you, the reader, understand how foreign it was for me to be sitting in a all black church.

CHAPTER 4

I was in a totally new world. I learned about a totally different kind of church. Pastors Vicks church was not about color, it was about God and saving souls. I took to it like a fish to water.

To sum it up I learned that all of life is basically a battle of good versus evil. God versus Satan. I also learned the power of scripture and bought the first Bible I had ever owned.

The Catholic Church read scriptures every mass and then the priest gives a sermon summarizing the scripture. I heard scripture all my life but I never understood the power in the word of the bible. I also never understood that Satan wanted my soul to burn in hell. That he was God's favorite angel and had been kicked from heaven when he began to believe that he was better than God. Wow, what a eye opener for a small town boy who only knew Catholicism.

In the beginning of this journey I learned how to pray. I mean really pray. I learned how to pray against evil and how to pray for healing. I learned the power of prayer. In my house growing up we always said blessing before meals and prayed at night before bed, but this type of prayer was vastly different than the way I was raised. I learned how to love and understand people.

In the spring of 1998, I was re-baptized in a cheap plastic kids swimming pool in the rear yard of the Church of God of Prophecy in Hammond. Pastor Vicks dunked my head under the water herself. I was clean from sin and had dedicated my soul to Jesus. I now fully understood that Jesus Christ had died on the cross for my sins and through him and his suffering my sins would be forgiven. I was born again.

I began to travel with Pastor Vicks to small churches and even to peoples homes where she preached.

Always the services built to a crescendo where the Holy Spirit would come in and move people.

One night in Plaquemine, Louisiana in a small black church the music was playing, I had my eyes closed and was singing. Pastor Vicks called me to the front of the church and asked me was I filled with the Holy Spirit.

I said I knew the feeling of the Holy Spirit at the services and prayer meetings we attended and that I could definitely feel when the Holy Spirit moved.

She said, "I know that you know what the Holy Spirit feels like but God has told me it's time for you to be filled with the Holy Spirit."

She called forward several members and asked them to lay hands on me. They did and I closed my eyes and they prayed over me asking God to fill me.

I was literally blown away. The next thing I knew I woke up on the floor with the church members all kneeling around me and I felt amazing, loved and as if I was surrounded by light. There is no drug or alcohol on this planet that can make a human feel the way I felt then.

On our drive home Pastor Vicks asked me to describe what had happened.

I told her that I truthfully did not remember. I remembered them laying hands on me and feeling the presence of the Holy spirit. Then I woke up on the floor, in near ecstasy.

She asked me if I remembered saying anything and I told her I did not.

She then told me that I had collapsed and began shouting in tongues and that I continued to shout in tongues for several minutes. She said the Holy Spirit was so powerful and it was truly a beautiful moment.

I had seen many people speak in tongues including Pastor Vicks when the Holy Spirit moved at different times. I had never understood it and in the beginning I doubted that it was real and not just people putting on a show for the church.

As time went on I had accepted people speaking in tongues and I could almost tell when it was going to happen because it would be a part of the service where I could feel the love and joy of the Holy Spirit moving.

It's like the service would start out slow with praise songs and then build and build until the Holy Spirit would move through the room touching everyone. Every time this happened it was a powerful and beautiful experience.

That night in Plaquemine, Pastor Vicks explained I had been slain in the power of the Holy Spirit. I knew she was right. Truthfully words cannot describe that feeling. I still cannot accurately describe it except to say it was beautiful and truly a gift from God.

All of this was so different from Catholicism and the way I was raised. I am not knocking Catholicism or any other religion. I know my mother gets the same peaceful feeling from going through the ritual of mass as I was getting those days at services and prayer meetings.

The difference for me was I had a relationship with Jesus. I felt connected to him through the Holy Spirit, by praying and reading the bible and being involved in spiritual warfare.

I now knew that when bad things happened it was because Satan was trying to attack.

CHAPTER 5

In time God would change the direction of my career and I would move on and away from the daily involvement of Pastor Vicks church, but I always carried my faith.

In the years to follow I would often times be led to bring people that were going through troubles and trials to Pastor Vicks so that she could pray for them. She was and is a powerful woman of God who dedicates her entire life to serving and praying for others and most importantly winning souls for Jesus and battling Satan. I pray everyday that the Lord will protect her and give her the strength to continue to fight Satan and his minions.

The purpose of this book is not for me to preach. I sin everyday. I am certainly no better than anyone else.

The only difference is because of Pastor Vicks I have a relationship with Jesus and I pray for those that do not.

I moved away from Pastor Vicks and her church as my law enforcement career progressed and I moved to another parish.

I immersed myself in my law enforcement career. One old veteran that I had known for years told me that when I started in law enforcement I should try to keep at least one friend that was a civilian as most cops end up spending all of their off duty time with other cops. He further stated that the cop life was more of a brotherhood and that keeping a civilian as a close friend could help a cop stay grounded.

As I surrounded myself with cops and immersed myself in the brotherhood I began to drink beer and party as a way to fellowship with my brothers and to blow off steam and stress from the job. I was single and enjoyed chasing women and I lived my life for me. I did this even though I had known a period while being active in Pastors Vicks church that I could not force my self to drink alcohol as I had lost all taste for it. Even now I could never be a alcoholic as I hate the feeling of being hung over. I however did enjoy having fun with friends and enjoyed my physical life.

CHAPTER 6

Fast forward many years later. I was a veteran law enforcement detective by this time and had transferred from the sheriff's office where I worked in detectives to the Louisiana State Police as a Criminal Investigator. I was also and still am a state licensed and board certified Polygraphist. I was assigned to the Internal Affairs Division for the Louisiana State Police which was a nice change from working with rapist, murderers and pedophiles.

I had been through a horrible divorce in which the devil tried to destroy me. I kept my head up and fought through it, knowing that when I was done with that battle God had a huge blessing for me.

You see, I know that the higher your spiritual level the bigger your devil. The more you turn to God the more Satan fights you.

I equate Satan to a deer hunter. When a person doesn't know Jesus or chooses sin over Jesus then Satan doesn't have to work hard to win their soul. He therefore spends more time and energy trying to destroy those who devote themselves to God. Satan is a master at warfare and knows just where your weaknesses are. He attacks you in the areas that you are most vulnerable. When Satan gets someone to turn from God while he is attacking them it is like a hunter killing a trophy buck. Whereas when he gets the soul of a person who denies God the kill would be equal to a hunter killing a small doe. The hunter would get meat from both deer but the trophy buck has the horns and bragging rights.

It is my personal belief that the closer you are to God the harder the devil fights to turn you away from him. Satan tries to knock you down spiritually because when you are attacked your human side takes over and you react through fear or anger like any human being would and you cannot be blessed by Jesus until you turn that battle over to him. Through prayer, and Jesus' grace and love you will ultimately be delivered from that battle. Upon your deliverance Jesus will once again be able to bless you and you once again move closer to him. When you reach victory through Jesus over that battle then that is what I call a higher level in Christ.

When Satan attacks us he hits hard. Let's say he attacks you through your spouse by enticing them to commit adultery. Anyone who loved their spouse will be crushed and filled with anger, hatred and consumed by the sadness and other emotions that are human and not of Jesus.

During this time of attack when we think of revenge, hate or anger we are acting on human emotions like any human being would because its in our nature, and that's just what Satan wants.

He wants to turn to God at that time and brag and say, "You see God they don't truly have faith. They are filled with emotions that have nothing to do with you! Look how they love to go to church and act pious and say how they are Christians. Now adversity comes and they crumble and give in to human emotions."

Now when we do this whether it is a cheating spouse, sickness, jealousy, financial problems, problems with family members or what ever the challenge we may face during the time when we are in our darkness of human emotions we cannot be blessed by God.

This is when faith comes in. Those that have or proclaim to have faith who succumb to the human emotions of the attacks cannot be blessed. When you are consumed in fear, anger or any emotion not of Jesus, whatever it is that you succumb to is like a huge umbrella you hold over your head that blocks any blessings or relief from God.

When we finally turn situation over to God, the umbrella is removed, then the blessings and the victory over the attack can rain down on you.

Saying you have faith or having faith in good times is easy. Learning how to recognize the attacks from Satan and to call them what they are and then exercising your faith and calling upon God or Jesus and the Holy Spirit to show you what to do to deliver you from the situation is a powerful thing. Knowing and believing that Jesus will deliver you is faith.

CHAPTER 7

So after my divorce and moving to the Louisiana State Police I met and fell in love with my wife, Cyndi. I had known her since we were young teenagers and, in fact, in high school she dated my best friend and I dated hers. We spent countless hours together growing up and then we both moved away and lived separate lives before coming back together again. We fell in love and quickly married.

We moved back to that same small town where we had grown up and were expecting our first child together. Cyndi was five months pregnant when this story began.

Cyndi and I were watching a movie in our living room the Monday after Easter Sunday. As we were watching the movie I began to have a pain in the back of my head behind my left ear. I felt the spot and noticed there was a bump that had never been there before. As the movie went on the bump and my pain both began to grow. When the movie was over the bump had turned into a visible knot and my pain level had skyrocketed and continued to grow worse.

I asked Cyndi to come and look at it. She first felt the bump and was amazed by its size. I had her take a picture of it with her phone and she showed it to me. You could clearly see a raised area on the back of my head about the size of a quarter. Had we known what was going to happen I would have saved that photograph for this book.

Cyndi was concerned as she knows I have a very high tolerance for pain. She also knows that I distrust hospitals and doctors as I had told her what happened to me in

2001.

In 2001, I sustained a head injury one night and did not seek medical attention for it. I slept all the next day.

I was working uniform patrol for the sheriff's office and was scheduled to go on duty at 6 pm. When 5 pm came I could not get out of bed. I was dizzy and in extreme pain.

Finally, I called the sheriff's office dispatch center. I was very close to the dispatchers I worked with. One of my dear friends, Tonya, answered the dispatch line.

I told her I needed her to send an ambulance to take me to the hospital. I knew that I was hurt very badly then.

Tonya and Brent (another sheriff office employee) actually left dispatch and came and brought me to the hospital themselves.

After a ridiculously long time of suffering and waiting in the emergency room I was sent for an x-ray and CT-scan. After even a longer amount of time the ER doctor came back and said there was nothing broken and maybe I had a slight concussion. He then told me if it did not get better in a week to contact my primary care physician. He gave me a prescription for pain pills, which I had filled.

Tonya and Brent brought me back to my apartment. I took a pain pill and it made me sick to my stomach. The rest of that week I laid in bed in severe pain. My balance was off and my ears had a constant ringing.

On the second day the phone in my bedroom rang and I answered it.

The male voice said, " Woody, this is Willie."

I was very agitated and said, "Willie who?" in a clearly angry voice.

He responded, "Willie Graves, your sheriff and boss, I was just calling to check on you."

I did not know at the time that people with serious head injuries are often angry and can sometimes become violent.

The sheriff told me to take as long as I needed to heal and he could see that I was in no mood to talk. Sheriff Graves also told me he would have deputies stop by and check on me.

It meant a lot to me that the sheriff would take the time to call and show his concern. I am still thankful to this day to Sheriff Graves for so many different things. He is a true Christian and I firmly believe God led me to work for him.

That week went by and I had a steady stream of visitors. Cops take care of their own.

I do not remember most of the week as I was bed ridden and in pain. I know that my friends fed me and were constantly checking on me. I also knew that physically something was very wrong with me.

The following Monday I had a sheriff's office friend drive me to Dr. John Piker's office which was located in the same town I grew up in.

Dr. John was a life long friend of my family and he took me in immediately. He checked my eyes and said that I needed a MRI done, as soon as possible. He left the room to schedule it and came back with the news that I would have to wait a week for the exam as that was the soonest they could see me.

He prescribed a non-narcotic pain medicine because I had told him that the previous prescription made me nauseous. My friend returned me to my apartment where I spent another week in severe pain. I was constantly dizzy and my ears rang non stop. I spent that week in bed.

The next Monday another sheriff's office friend drove me to my MRI appointment. I was still very sick and in a lot of pain. When I finished the MRI they told me it would be over a week until I could get the results. I couldn't comprehend having to suffer another week before finding out what was wrong. Again, I was returned home.

The following week, on a Friday, I was notified that the results were ready. Again, a sheriff's office friend drove me to pick up the results and then we drove the hour back to Dr. John Piker's office only to find that he was closed on Fridays. I returned home and continued to suffer until Monday.

On Monday my sheriff's office friend again drove me the hour to Dr. John's office. He took me in immediately to read the results of the MRI.

As soon as he looked at them he said, "We have to get you to a neurosurgeon now."

Dr. John had to call several neurosurgeons until he found one that could see me that day.

My friend drove me to the neurosurgeon's office. When the doctor entered the room I handed him the MRI results; he was shocked. The doctor said he could not believe I had made it on my own for four weeks. The doctor then informed me that I had a very serious brain injury. He told me that my left temporal bone was fractured and that I had two large subdural hematoma's on my brain.

In layman's terms my skull was broken and I had two spots on my brain that were bleeding. The doctor wanted to put me in the hospital right away and said that I might need surgery.

I objected. I asked the doctor why couldn't I just return home. I further asked, if I had not died in a month why would I die now? He explained that the hemotoma's were large bruises on my brain that were where my brain had bled. He stated that my brain would either continue to bleed and I would die or over time the brain would heal and reabsorb the blood from the hemotoma's.

I asked what the treatment would be. He said he would admit me to the hospital where they could monitor me and if the brain didn't start to heal they would have to do surgery to release the swelling.

I refused to be hospitalized and stated that I had been incapacitated by pain for a month after having the emergency room doctor tell me that there was nothing wrong with my head after he had reviewed CT-scan and x-ray results.

I mean really? How do you miss a fractured skull?

I wasn't going to be admitted. The doctor said that he wanted me to have another MRI done ASAP. His office scheduled it. Guess what?-- the first appointment they could get was another week away. I declined the doctors offer for pain medication and returned home for another week of pain, dizziness and head ringing.

The following week (5 weeks after injury) I had another MRI. I had to wait another week for the doctor to get the results and for my appointment.

So 6 weeks after the injury the neurosurgeon and I meet again. He advises me that the bleeding had not grown any and seemed to have shrunk a little.

He again wanted to put me in the hospital and I refused. He scheduled another MRI for the following week and a appointment with him to follow the week after that.

After 8 weeks of being home alone I was once again in the neurosurgeons office and he told me that my brain was healing and it would take time. Ultimately it was 16 weeks before he released me to go back to work, on light duty, and then probably another four weeks before I was cleared to return to uniform patrol.

The point of my telling you about the 20 weeks I spent suffering and recovering is two fold.

First, it shows you partially why I distrust doctors and hospitals. That ER doctor told me there was nothing wrong with me and that I might have a slight concussion.

Really? Somehow he didn't see my fractured skull in the CT-scan or x-ray?

The second reason is to show you that I truly do have a very high pain tolerance level as I spent that first month at deaths door and still refused narcotic pain medications.

Thank God that I cannot truly remember how bad the pain was during that time.

CHAPTER 8

So I am sitting in my recliner ten years after being healed from the head injury. The pain I'm feeling is growing by the minute. It became so intense that I began to feel nauseous. Cyndi was very concerned and I didn't tell her but I was growing more scared every minute as the pain continued to grow. I went to the bathroom and began to throw up from the pain. Cyndi came in and wiped my forehead with a wet cloth and I asked her to just let me be for a few minutes.

In truth, I was about to pass out from the pain and Cyndi was 5 months pregnant and I didn't want to cause her anymore stress. So I sat on the floor in the bathroom in front of the toilet trying to slow my breathing and to get a grip on the pain that I was consuming me.

Finally, I stood and returned to the living room which was no easy feat. I again almost passed out. I thought if I could just sit for a bit maybe the pain would pass. I sat down and the pain escalated. It was blinding. I was seeing stars.

I then told Cyndi in a calm voice that if I passed out it was no big deal just for her to call 911 and get me a ambulance. I was trying to rationalize and endure the pain, hoping that it would pass.

After another 15 minutes I told Cyndi that she had to take me to the emergency room. I was beyond the point of trying to rationalize the pain. I knew something was seriously wrong.

The nearest emergency room from our rural home was at least thirty minutes away. I had always swore that I would never go to that emergency room as it had a reputation for killing people.

It's a small community hospital. Years earlier my best friends dad had gone there with shortness of breath and died in the emergency room a short time later. More recently my fathers best friend had gone in for a knee replacement and died on the operating table at the same hospital.

I think the only person more afraid of hospitals than me is my father and he made it clear that if something ever happened to him he wanted to be driven the extra 15 minutes to one of the bigger hospitals in Baton Rouge as he was afraid of being taken to this hospital.

When Cyndi was driving me I did not care what hospital we went to I just needed to get medical help and I needed it fast. She had to stop several times during the drive for me to throw up on the side of the road from the pain.

We arrived at the emergency room and after a very long wait I was escorted back to be examined.

I was put on an exam table and the medical staff asked all of the usual medical history questions, and symptoms. I could not answer them as every sound was causing me more pain.

Cyndi finally said, "Can't you do something for the pain?"

I will never forget what happened next.

I had a male nurse that was attending to me while the doctor was talking to Cyndi. The doctor ordered him to give me a shot of Dilaudid. I remember the male nurse looking at me as he prepared the needle to inject in my right arm.

He said, "Don't worry sir. I am going to give you a shot of the good stuff. In a minute you won't feel any pain, I promise."

He stated this while he was inserting the needle into my vein. I was watching in eager anticipation of having anything that could lessen my pain. The nurse started to plunge the Dilaudid into my vein and I could never have dreamed what would happen next.

As the Dilaudid entered my vein I could feel it. It began to burn like fire. I actually felt it as it flowed into my blood stream. As it moved through the vein in my arm it left behind a burning pain that I could not have imagined. It must have only been seconds but it felt like hours as the Dilaudid ran through my veins. I was so shocked by the pain that I couldn't speak. It first reached my right hand which instantly cramped involuntary into a claw. My fingers contracted into a fist that was on fire. Meanwhile, I could feel the medicine flowing up the vein in my arm. It burned like hell. I was shocked.

I could actually feel it as it went up my arm and my entire arm burned. Then it moved across my chest and towards my heart. I felt it as it burned its way across. I started crying and could not believe the intensity of the pain and then it reached my heart and throat at about the same time. I felt my heart contract and seize up.

I was able to say, "My chest." before my throat closed up.

At the same time I realized I am having a heart attack and I can't breath I can still feel the Dilaudid working its way through the rest of my body eventually reaching my feet. I had on open toe sandals and my toes involuntary curled up with cramps as the medicine hit them. All of this happened in a matter of seconds but from the time I felt the Dilaudid enter my arm to the time it reached my toes seemed like an eternity.

I just thought I had experienced pain that night before I decided to go to the hospital. Now I lay crying unable to speak and literally not breathing and my whole body was in a seized contracted state. The most painful of which was my heart which I knew was cramped and it had stopped beating. I knew I was dying.

CHAPTER 9

Back to my faith. Throughout my law enforcement career I had to deal with people who died. While working corrections I witnessed several people that had committed suicide. I cut down the body of one guy and tried to resuscitate him to no avail. In uniform patrol I often saw dead bodies. Most were from violent car crashes. The rest were from suicides, drug overdoses and homicides.

When I was promoted to detective death was a constant companion. Every death that is obviously not of natural causes has to be investigated until the cause of death is determined. This is especially important on accidental overdoses, accidental shootings, and suicides.

When I would get a call out to a death scene I treated everyone of them as a homicide until I could prove otherwise. Of course, some were homicide. I saw every type of homicide from a negligent shooting of another to cold blooded premeditated murder.

One thing almost all of the violent homicide victims had in common is that they were living what I call a high risk lifestyle. For example, a drug dealer shoots another drug dealer or a prostitute is strangled, etc.

I always wondered when I was looking at the body or bodies at a murder scene what the victim was thinking in their last seconds before death.

In some cases death had obviously taken a long time as in the case of a 82 year old lady that I worked who had 57 blunt force trauma blows to her head. The blows didn't kill her. This lady did not live a highrisk life style. She had in fact spent her life raising orphans and had many children and grand children and she was loved by all.

Her son in law was having sex with his wife's sister when the 82 year old walked in on them and saw them having sex and shooting up cocaine together. When she told them that she was going to call her other daughter and tell, they proceeded to beat her on the head with a glass coke bottle and a vase before leaving her on the floor in the hallway for what they thought was dead.

They returned to shooting up cocaine and having sex until one of them heard the 82 year old victim gurgling.

The male then went to his gun cabinet and took a 22 caliber rifle and bullets, loaded the gun, and went and stood over the victim in the hallway and put the rifle to her head and pulled the trigger.

Nothing happened and he realized he had put a 22 short caliber round in the rifle instead of a 22 long rifle. He then walked back down the hall through the blood and got the correct caliber and walked back through the blood again, stood over her and shot her in the back of the head one time.

The couple then pulled the 82 year old victims panties down and raised her nightgown in an attempt to make it look like a rape.

The victim never had a chance to get away because she used a walker.

I know the intimate details of this homicide because my partner and I got a full confession after a week of chasing the bad guy and we were able to prove the daughters part in the murder because her blood was found mixed with her mothers blood. Apparently she cut her self when the vase she was smashing her mothers head in with broke.

My point is this. Every death I ever worked I wondered at the last second when the victim realized that they were going to die if they called on Jesus, would he come for them. I especially wondered this about the victims who lived and died because of their high risk lifestyle. I was about to find out the answer to my question.

CHAPTER 10

In the last second when my whole body was on fire, and seized in one giant cramp, I could not breath or speak and my wife was trying to uncurl my toes as she could see they were knotted in a cramp.

I cried out in my mind, "Jesus help me!"

Instantly I felt someone take a hold on me from under my arms. It was as if the person was standing behind me and grabbed me under my arms and was attempting to pull me backwards. At the same time I clearly heard a male voice say, "I've got you."

Where I could feel the contact, where someone was pulling me back, I instantly felt the most beautiful feeling I had ever experienced. It was indescribable. You know the love you have for your children or the person you love most in this world? Where I was being held felt like that times infinity. More love than I could have ever dreamed existed. I knew that Jesus had answered my cry and that he was holding me.

At the same time I am looking down at my wife as she was trying desperately to do something to unclench my toes. I felt the excruciating pain and body seizure from my upper chest down to my toes. Where Jesus was holding and pulling my spirit backwards I felt the total love and ecstasy.

I knew instantly and without a doubt that Jesus was holding me. When I felt him holding me and heard him say "I've got You."

I cried out again to him in my mind and screamed "the pain!"

I clearly heard him state, "Its yours to bear for now."

I looked again at Cyndi who was five months pregnant and I cried out to Jesus, "My family!"

I clearly heard him say, "It's okay, I have you, its going to be okay."

I am overwhelmed. I have Jesus holding me and telling me its okay, he has me and that the pain was mine to bear for now. I feel more love than can be imagined and in my mind when Jesus said the pain is yours to bear for now I thought he meant he had come to take me to heaven and that I had to bear the pain until we left.

I was still feeling the death pain below and the love above where he was holding me. I knew I had a beautiful family to take care of but to be honest I was ready to go with Jesus. The feeling of him holding me was more important at that time than me remaining with my family or anything else.

I was able to speak out loud and I said, "Cyndi its okay. Jesus is here. Jesus is here and I am going to go with him now. I love you and I am going with Jesus. Jesus said everything is going to be okay."

Cyndi shouted, "Its not okay!" and jumped from my feet to my chest and grabbed me in a hug.

At that instant my connection to Jesus was lost.

Cyndi was holding on saying, "You can't go. You can't go."

Meanwhile the medical staff has freaked out. They are running around and shouting. The "crash cart" was brought beside me. I felt my muscles begin to unclench and my heart start to beat.

I was still having trouble breathing and it felt like my throat was swollen shut. They put an oxygen mask on me and when I could speak I told Cyndi to call my parents.

She dialed the number and my mother answered. I told her to wake my dad that I needed to talk to him. My dad came on the line and I told him where I was at and that I had just had a heart attack.

He said, "We are on our way."

I then told Cyndi to call Pastor Vicks. When Pastor Vicks got on the phone I told her that I had just had a heart attack and I was in emergency room.

She immediately began to pray against the devil and the attack I was under. I stopped her and said that that was not what I was calling for. I told her I wanted her to reaffirm that I was saved.

She then asked me if I believe in Jesus Christ as my savior.

I was crying and I said, "Yes I Do."

She then asked if I knew that Jesus had died on the cross for my sins.

I again responded, "Yes I do!" almost shouting while crying.

She asked me if I accepted Christ as the son of God and knew that he died on the cross for my sins.

I said, "Yes! Yes! Yes!"

I had just felt the glory of God himself and Jesus' total love as he held me when I called as I was dying.

I couldn't believe the love that I had felt from Jesus in that moment. It was beyond beautiful, beyond ecstasy.

Jesus had not only answered when I called but he held me and let me feel his total love.

Pastor Vicks said she was on her way to the hospital and that she would call other prayer warriors who were close to get them there to pray over me as she was over a hour away.

CHAPTER 11

It seemed like minutes while I lay there holding Cyndi and crying. The medical staff was preparing to move me for a CT-scan when my parents arrived and hugged me.

I was still crying as I told them what had happened when I was given the shot. Hospital staff came and stated that only two people could be with me, and that no one could come with me when I went for the CT-scan.

I told Cyndi to go out and call her mom. I was worried about the baby. I asked my mom to go with Cyndi and stay with her until my mother in law arrived.

They left as the medical staff was wheeling me for the CT-scan. My father came with me for the CT-scan even though they said he couldn't. He was holding my hand as I was still having trouble breathing and my mouth was so dry I could not swallow.

They wheeled me into the room and a technician came out. I begged him for water. He refused.

He stated, "I'm going to strap you down and put you in for the scan and its going to take approximately ten minutes."

I pleaded with him not to. I begged him for some water. I had never been so thirsty in my life. I would drag my teeth across my tongue in a attempt to draw out some kind of moisture. I was unsuccessful. My tongue was white and dry.

My poor father stood looking as they strapped me to the table against my repeated pleas not to put me in the machine before I had water. I could not swallow and that was one of the worst things I had ever experienced. Trying to swallow and not being able to because the throat muscles have no lubrication. I was on the verge of full blown panic when they put me in the machine and turned it on.

I felt as if I was choking to death. I was crying when I cried out again in my mind "JESUS" instantly I heard his voice say, "I thirst." Which is one of the last things he said on the Crucifixion Cross before his death.

Upon hearing his words my whole body felt his love again. The love I felt earlier when he held me under my arms. Instantly my thirst disappeared and I began to see visions of such beauty that I was astonished. I wish I could remember more but two I remember for sure.

The first was three golden crosses which were burning with the most beautiful fire I had ever seen. Even though I can still see them in my mind now I could never do justice to trying to describe their beauty.

The second one I remember is seeing Cyndi and I walking along a star lit beautiful beach holding hands. The water sparkled from the stars and the moonlight. The trees were tall palms like the ones in the pacific. I am a avid diver and I am certain it was like no place I had ever visited in the Caribbean.

More importantly what I saw was that Cyndi and I were old, like in our late 80's, gray haired and walking hand in hand. It was so beautiful.

I saw many more visions during the eight or so minutes I was in the CT-scan but I cannot recall specific details. I can tell you that I was being held by Jesus and it was unbelievable. The joy I felt was and is indescribable. The visions came rapid fire and were so awesome and mind blowing!

By the time the CT-scan was over I was able to swallow and had no more pain from the reaction to the Dilaudid shot. They wheeled me back to the room and my father stayed with me holding my hand until Cyndi returned. This speaks volumes to my dad's character as he is the only person who hates hospitals more than me. He stood beside me in my darkest hour like a rock, I hope I will always be there for my children like my parents were that night.

CHAPTER 12

It took sometime before the results from the CT-scan came back. While we waited, Cyndi had contacted our lifelong friend who was the girlfriend of the Supervising Chief Doctor of the Emergency Room.

Her parents and my parents had been best of friends for over forty years. The doctor was with the friend and they told him of my situation.

The emergency room doctor took this time to come back in and tell me that there was nothing wrong with me.

Yep, that's right. He told me that there was nothing wrong with me. I was floored. I still had the pain which I had come to the emergency room for although it had taken a back seat to me dying on the table after the shot of Dilaudid.

I told the doctor that the knot on the back of my head was certainly wrong and that I had felt it come up over the period of two hours.

He explained that was simply impossible. The doctor then proceeded to tell me that the bump on the back of my head was a fatty lipoma and had to have been there for years.

I again told him that I had felt it come up that night, Cyndi even showed the time lapsed pictures and I could guarantee him that it had not been there for years. He again stated that I was wrong and that the bump would not cause pain and that it had developed over years, not in one night.

I started to get pissed. I then asked about my reaction to the Dilaudid shot and he said it was all in my mind and that I had had a panic attack.

Now I was getting really mad. I told him what I had experienced was not a panic attack. He again disagreed.

My parents and my wife were just as dumbfounded as me. The doctor had a attitude. He was being rude and short with his answers. The more we tried to find out what happened the shorter his answers became.

I then had Cyndi hand him the phone. He at first refused it saying there was no one he needed to talk to but when he was told it was the emergency room supervising doctor he was shocked.

Talk about a demeanor change. I heard him answer the questions of his supervisor.

"Yes, sir. Yes, doctor. Yes,sir."

When he handed the phone back he was really mad.

He again stated that the knot on the back of my head was nothing and that I had a panic attack. He referred me to an ENT doctor in the morning and released me with some pain medications.

Can you believe that? I went from literally dying on that table (by dying I mean I could not breath and a crash cart was next to my side because my heart had stopped) to being given some pain pills, and released to see another doctor in the morning.

CHAPTER 13

Technically, it was already morning as it was now around 4 am. I was mad at the doctor but at the same time I had never been so excited in my entire life.

You see, I had always believed in Jesus and my faith had grown throughout my life. But now I knew Jesus and God were real. Jesus had held me! I heard him and felt his true and overpowering love.

He came when I called in my darkest hour, not once but twice and showed me true love that no human words can describe. There are literally not enough words in any language to adequately describe being held by God.

Praise Jesus!

What I didn't know is that when Jesus told me the pain was mine to bear for now was that these were my first hours on a journey that would take me to the depths of mental and physical hell.

My wife drove us back to our house and although I was still in severe pain it was not as bad as it had been before going to the emergency room because they had given me some pain pills.

It didn't matter. What a contradiction, the pain I was in was nothing compared to the high I was on from knowing that Jesus had held me and knowing without a doubt that he was and is real. I could not stop talking about it.

We had a appointment in just a few hours with a ENT doctor and I didn't sleep at all. I was on my knees praying and giving thanks to Jesus for what he had done. I felt richer than the richest man on earth.

I knew I had died and I knew that Jesus came for me and the love and joy of his presence was mind boggling and overwhelming. The visions he showed me were of such beauty and color that I could never accurately describe them. I don't think some of the colors even exist on this planet.

I wish I had written all that I could describing Jesus love and what he showed me that night when I got back from the hospital. I guess God didn't want me to remember everything or I would have.

I had no clue what was about to happen.

CHAPTER 14

A few hours later Cyndi drove me to Dr. Surek's office in Zachary, Louisiana. I said I would not mention specific doctors or hospitals by name as I am not trying to call them out on the bad that they did but Dr. Surek is different, as the story goes along you will see why.

We arrived at the office and his waiting room was packed. I was hurting and I truly do not remember how long it was until he saw us. We were ushered back to a exam room, a nurse took all of the usual information, Cyndi filled out the forms and they checked my temperature and blood pressure.

Finally, Dr. Surek came in and he was wearing the white coat with a stethoscope around his neck. He was probably five foot ten or so and had dirty blonde curly hair and a nice smile.

We explained how the bump came up on the back of my head and caused the pain which led to the emergency room trip, my allergic reaction to Dilaudid and what happened next.

I told him about Jesus holding me and the love and grace I experienced. He did not laugh or make fun of me. He listened very intently and I could tell that my experience touched him. He explained that he was a deacon in the Catholic Church and he totally believed God would do that for me.

Dr. Surek then examined me and asked questions about the pain and felt the knot on my head. When I explained how bad the pain was, my high tolerance for pain and that I had never been to the doctor, as an adult, except for when I had fractured my skull in 2001, he listened.

When I finished speaking he said that I needed to be admitted to the hospital right away. He said I could not go home to get clothes or delay in anyway. He called the hospital himself, wrote the order for me to be admitted and said that they had to find out what was wrong. He explained that there would be many test run on me and that he would be handing me over to a neurologist and a pain doctor.

We thanked him and went immediately to the hospital which was in Baton Rouge after refusing the one connected to the emergency room from the night before.

CHAPTER 15

Now this is where I will tell you how my experience began to go downhill fast. I have always detested hospitals. In working as a major crime detective I have spent a lot of time in hospitals talking to victims of violent crimes and interviewing witnesses which included doctors. My experiences as a detective did nothing to further my trust for hospitals and doctors. I'll take a minute to give you an example of one of the many bad experiences I had with them.

One Sunday I was the detective on call and was dispatched to a case that was a supposed overdose. The residence was approximately 40 minutes travel time from my location and I drove as fast as I could to get there.

Upon my arrival I observed Acadian Ambulance loading a white female on a stretcher into the ambulance. I immediately went to ask what they were doing. I had been told that the female was found dead by her step father.

The paramedic said they had been told the same but upon their arrival they had found a slight pulse and they were taking her to the emergency room.

As chance would have it it was the same emergency room that I went to in 2001 where they had missed the fact that my brain was bleeding in two places and that my skull was fractured.

This was not out of the ordinary as I often went to this emergency room as a detective because it was the closest one to that rural area where I worked.

I told them that we would be there as soon as we processed the scene. Remember we treated every death as a homicide until we could prove otherwise.

My partner and I entered the residence and interviewed the girls stepfather who stated that he worked the night shift at a plant as a machinist and that when he got home that morning around 6am he went into his stepdaughters room to see if she was alright. He said he entered the her room and saw her with the covers pulled up to her chin. He said she was sleeping so he exited the room and went to bed and awoke around 2pm.

He said when he awoke he noticed that the stepdaughters infant baby was still in her crib but was standing up and crying.

I asked where his wife was and he explained that she was in a hospital with third degree burns on her body. He stated that she had been burning wood in the back yard and spilled gas on herself and caught on fire. So for the last few weeks he and the victim had been living alone in the residence.

The stepfather appeared to be in his mid-fifties and was overweight and had thick glasses. He was not a attractive man. I had been observing the residence while he had been speaking to us and noticed pictures of the victim and she was truly beautiful. She was approximately 19 had long blonde hair and the face and body of a model.

He stated that when he saw the baby in the crib crying he went to his stepdaughters room and opened the door and that he then saw her lying on the floor. He said she was dead.

I asked him how he knew she was dead and he stated that he just knew. He stated he then called 911 and told the dispatcher they needed to send someone as his stepdaughter was dead.

The ambulance driver told me when they arrived the stepfather told them there was no need to hurry because she was dead and that she needed a hearse not a ambulance.

Now 98.5 percent of what I do for a living is read people, and I knew this guy was trouble. I knew right away that he had something to do with the victims condition and there was several reasons why I felt this way. I continued to ask him basic straightforward questions in a non accusatory way to lock him into his story of exactly what had happened since he had returned home that morning. I recorded the entire conversation.

Finally, I asked him what he thought had happened to her and he stated that she had a pain pill addiction and that she called him the night before at his work and asked if she could have a few friends over. He said no and she became angry with him. He stated that he believed she must have had friends over and then she overdosed.

I knew he was full of it but we processed the scene as normal taking photographs etc. I was not going to confront him further until I went to the hospital and talked to the doctors about her condition.

My partner and I left and went to the emergency room. We were cleared through security into the back part of the emergency room which held all of the exam and trauma rooms. They were extremely busy and we asked to see the victim. Neither my partner or I had seen her up close before she was loaded into the ambulance due to the fact of our response time and that they were rushing her to the hospital.

The emergency room nurse told us that she probably wasn't going to make it. We asked to see her and they made us wait. The doctor came out of the room. He stated unsolicited that there was no need for us to see her as it was a obvious overdose and the girl would not live. He stated that they were working on her and that the room was overcrowded.

I explained that I at least needed to photograph her and he said, "No, you can't go in."

This doctor was in his mid forties and was being very short with us.

I then asked the doctor if there were any visible signs of injury on the female victim.

He said, "No there are no injuries. She is a drug head and it's an overdose and I don't have time to stand here and talk."

I asked him if he had examined her for injuries to the body and he said he had examined her. She didn't have any and that it was a overdose and that the interview was over.

My partner and I left and I told him I thought the step-dad was lying. I believed that something was going on and that his story did not add up.

My first reason for my belief was that he said he went into her room to check on her at 6am and that she was sleeping in the bed with the covers up to her neck. I found it strange that a grown man would come home after working all night and that the first thing he does is to go check on his adult stepdaughter. He didn't just crack the door and see that she was sleeping. He made the fact clear that he went into the bedroom and stood over her and observed that the blankets were up to her neck. Why would he check on an adult? If he checked on her he could certainly see from a cracked door that she was asleep, in the bed, and there was no need for him to go into the room, stand over her and see that the blankets were pulled up to her neck. It just bothered me. It didn't feel right.

My partner was a older detective and he said, "It is what it is. The doctor says it's an overdose, then that's it. The doctor said he examined her for injuries and there were none, so we are done. She overdosed. End of story."

CHAPTER 16

The next day my partner and I were off duty after having worked the weekend shift. I was at home and my pager went off displaying a message which told me to call him as soon as possible.

I called him and he stated that the hospitals' ICU called and wanted to know if we were going to come work the case on our victim. My partner told them the case was closed as the doctor had stated it was a overdose.

The ICU chief told my partner that the victim had been beat to hell and that we needed to come and take photographs of the injuries.

We responded to the hospitals ICU and were escorted into her room by the ICU doctor and two nurses.

I could not believe what I saw. The victim had bruises and scratches all over her. Back then we still used Polaroid cameras. I had the doctor point out every injury he had found during his exam of the victim. I ended up taking 62 different pictures of the victims body. She had been beat and scratched every where. It was truly a sad sight. This beautiful young lady had been severely traumatized and was now on life support in the ICU.

I asked the doctor how the emergency room doctor could tell us that she had no injuries and that it was just another overdose. He had no answer.

He did state that the injuries were over 24 hours old and that he could tell because of the state of the bruises and scratches. He would not speculate about the emergency room doctor.

One thing I have found throughout my career and private life is doctors generally stick together and it is almost impossible to get one to say something bad about another. I was very angry. I knew I should have gone on my gut instinct and demanded to photograph the victim the day before. I knew the step-dad was lying and I had let a emergency room doctor influence me as well as a veteran detective who was just glad that it wasn't a homicide so that he could get off duty and not have his days off interrupted. He knew that if it was foul play we would be working nonstop to solve the case. Now we were getting a late start and looked like idiots.

We returned to the residence and met with the step-dad. Now was my time to ask what I should have the day before. I asked him to tell what happened again and he gave his same story verbatim.

I then asked why a man goes into his adult stepdaughters room to check on her when he got home. I followed that with questions about why he felt the need to say the blankets were up to her neck and why he had not tried to resuscitate her and why he told everyone she was dead. I asked him many questions and then confronted him with the photographs of the victims injuries. He then asked for a lawyer.

To sum this case up about a week or so later the ICU called and said we needed to come back. Upon our arrival the doctor explained that they had done a some type of test and determined that the victim was getting air into her skull in some way. They then went to the base of her skull and found a hole that had gone unnoticed previously because the hole had been covered by her long hair. It was a perfect round puncture wound that appeared to be from some type of injection.

When the victims blood work came back she was found to have Acetone injected into that site. Yes, acetone or paint remover.

I prepared a search warrant and we went back to the residence and found a used can of acetone and a Cajun injector syringe in an outside garage. I ultimately got the step-dad to admit to sexual battery of the victim while she was sleeping, he stated that he just couldn't help himself that she was too pretty.
He waived his right to a lawyer when I got this taped confession.

The victim ended up dying a year later in a extended care home. She never regained consciousness.

At her autopsy she weighed less than 70 pounds and had bed sores.

As far as I know the District Attorney has never sought to further the prosecution for her murder. I know this is because a good defense attorney would state that the injection and injuries could have occurred at the hospital after she had been admitted.

So again by trusting an emergency room doctor I had been screwed.

I know that the step-dad is guilty and he does also that's why he ended up confessing to the sexual battery of his stepdaughter. But because we had been turned away by the ER doctor the murder case was in jeopardy as the defense could not only say that she had been beaten and injected in the hospital but that whoever beat her and injected her with acetone would have had plenty of time and opportunity to go to that residence and plant the acetone and needle in the shed. Lesson learned for me ---- I was never going to trust any doctor again. The step dad plead guilty to sexual battery and was sentenced to a short prison term.

CHAPTER 17

My wife and I go through the admission process and the full hospital experience begins. First volumes of paperwork. Then getting a room. Followed by a steady stream of nurses and doctors. The first doctor came in and I told him about the bump. He too said the bump could not have come up that fast. It was just a fatty lipoma that had been there for years. Sound familiar? Now this doctor was a widely respected Neurosurgeon and he is totally dismissing the fact that I am telling him I felt it come up on my head less than 24 hours before and that is when the pain started. At that time, I had pictures that showed the bumps progress over a few hours.

"Nope, it couldn't have happened that way" ,he said.

He then tells them to give me Dilaudid for the pain after my IV is started. Cyndi and I both tell him of the allergic reaction I had the night before.

 He responded, "No, you just panicked."

Does this sound familiar? At this time I am suffering so bad I go against my better judgment and again let a doctor sway my good sense and agree to let the nurse do it.

She said for me to turn my head the opposite direction while she started my IV and that she would go slow when administering the Dilaudid because sometimes the Dilaudid is administered too fast and can cause discomfort.

I told her what I felt was not discomfort it had been death. I turned my head and waited, and waited, and waited. I kept feeling sticks in my arm from the needle. Turns out she could not get the IV started. She had to call another nurse who tries several times and she can't get it started.

Keep in mind my head is killing me. I am almost to the point of tears from the pain even though I had been given Lortab earlier when they admitted me. They keep sticking me and it hurts but its nothing compared to the pain in my head which is exasperated by the very sound of people talking and the light in the room. The pain continued to grow.

Almost thirty minutes later, no one can get the IV started so they call in the head nurse and she tries umpteen times on different veins on my hands and arms with no success.

It's a circus in the room as all of these medical professionals gather to gaze at the wonder of the patient that not even the head nurse can start an IV on correctly.

Finally, they call the head emergency room nurse. He arrives and its standing room only as everyone wants to watch him work his magic and to his credit he did get the needle to go in after several tries to some obscure vein on my right arm.

I was about to cry from the pain. So the original nurse tells me to turn my head as she administered the Dilaudid. I turned my head and she continued talking to my wife and told me I would not even know when the medicine was going in that she was going to go really slow.

A few seconds passed and I felt it again. My arm started to cramp and was on fire just as it had the night before in the emergency room. It was not spreading as rapid as the shot in the emergency room but it was spreading.

I said, "Stop. Stop. Stop."

I was in fear that it would lead to another heart stoppage and choking cramping experience that I had the night before.

The nurse was shocked.

She said, "I just started to push and had not even probably pushed a whole drop in when you started reacting."

Thankfully, the pain didn't spread throughout my body this time. The cramping made it no further than my arm. Once again though I suffered, even though it was for seconds. I suffered at the hands of a medical professional who simply would not believe what I told them.

She went to the doctor and told him that I was indeed allergic to Dilaudid so they switched to Morphine and it burned where they injected it but did not run through my body like the Dilaudid had and the Morphine did provide some pain relief. It certainly did not stop the pain but brought it down enough where I could open my eyes and that sounds in the room didn't hurt my head as bad.

The morphine was not enough though. I could tell you exactly when it started to wear off. After about three hours the pain would begin to intensify again and I would have Cyndi call the nurses to tell them but I could not have anymore until the four hours was up. That last hour I would begin crying as the pain increased as the minutes passed.

That first night was really bad as they wouldn't even give me Tylenol to help with the last hour when the pain would again begin to increase. Remember that the Morphine did not kill the pain or make me high. It just made it bearable to the point that I wasn't puking and crying.

CHAPTER 18

The next morning the neurosurgeon came in and examined me again. I tell him about the pain and he prescribed pain pills to be taken in between the Morphine doses.

I explained that the Morphine really didn't do much more than to bring the pain from a 10 to maybe a 9. He said lets try tonight and see how it goes. The pain pills helped and maybe brought the pain with the Morphine from a 9 to an 8 3/4. I knew exactly when they started to wear off and every time the pain became blinding and crippling until they gave me the next shot of Morphine.

Lord help me when the nurse was late because of helping another person. This pain cannot be adequately described it was so intense that I literally thought I would either die or go crazy from it. In fact, it was so intense the slightest breeze on my face was excruciating. Cyndi could not walk by my side or move in the room for fear of a breeze from her movement hitting me.

The next day the neurologist exams me again. When I tell him of the pain and that I know exactly when the medications are wearing off and how it makes me feel like I am dying or going to lose my mind he calls in a pain medicine doctor.

This doctor examines me and consults with the neurologist and he loads me up. I still have a list of all the medications I was prescribed, the day they were prescribed, the dosage amount and times to take them. But it doesn't matter, I can tell you it would alternate like every hour. Morphine then some pain pill like Lortab about two hours later then Oxycontin then another type of pain pill that was opposite of the Lortab then back to the morphine. All in all it brought my pain from a 10 to maybe a 7 1/2. Much better but I was still incapacitated. I could not walk so they put a catheter in me.

Every morning the neurologist would show early and examine me and then order the test for that day. I was certainly not laying in the bed all day resting. I cannot tell you how many MRI or CT-scans I had done but it was a lot. I lost count.

Plus x-rays and constant blood work. There were tests where they injected dyes into me to study different areas of me. The doctors were at a loss. No one had a clue. They had never seen anything like this before and could not explain it.

Two weeks went by. Two weeks in the hospital is forever. Hospitals kill people, of that I am convinced. If you ever want to go to a place where you can never sleep for more than a hour and a half go check into a hospital.

Not only was I being awoken every two hours by the nurses coming in to give me pain medications, I was also awoken at any random time by food service, housekeeping, and anything else you can think of.

You would think a hospital could get better organized. I mean I understand food coming three times a day. I also understand the tray and leftovers being removed from the room. But each shift would send in housekeeping at no certain time. I mean its like 3am and a guy comes in to change out the trash bag. Later another person comes and sweeps and mops the floor. Every four hours regardless if its medicine time or not some nurse comes in and takes your temperature and blood pressure. It never stopped and I was going crazy. One day when I thought I was going to get some rest a hospital worker comes in and wants us to fill out a survey on my hospital stay. It was never ending.

CHAPTER 19

One thing cops do is take care of one another. When a cop goes in the hospital you will never find him or her alone. Cops come and go at different hours as most work shift work. Also, my family and friend base was huge. So people were always coming to knock on the door to visit. That lasted for about a day as I was in so much pain I could not talk and I could not have the light on in the room. The smallest noise made my head scream no matter how much pain medicine I was on and my sense of smell had grown so strong that the slightest scent would gag me. Cyndi had the nurse put a no visitor sign and a do not knock sign on the door. Luckily my room was at the end of the hall and I did not have to hear a lot of hall noise. I appreciate everyone who tried to see me, but I couldn't, I just was physically and mentally unable.

The one person who never left me was my wife, Cyndi. She stayed every night and everyday and only left twice to go to the cafeteria in two weeks when my parents came to visit.

I guess they didn't come to visit as much as to just sit with me for a few minutes as they knew talking was out of the question.

Cyndi ate what I did not eat from my hospital food. For two weeks she sat in the dark and watched over me like a hawk. She made notes of every single person and doctor or nurse that came and what medicine I was given at what time, what I ate, when I slept, everything. All the while she was sleeping in a chair bed, and don't forget she was 5 months pregnant with our son. I don't know of anyone else who could have stood that time. My wife is one tough lady.

CHAPTER 20

So during the two weeks I never turned on the television in the room because of the pain the noise and light would cause. One night I turned it on at 10 pm to watch the news.

I am a news junkie and I hadn't seen it in at least a week. I turned on the news and the lead story was that a Baton Rouge City police officer had been killed in a fiery crash on Interstate 10 outside of Baton Rouge.

I know a lot of Baton Rouge City officers and when the news story started and the announcer stated that the officer was Russel Kiger I was blown away. Russel was one of my best and dearest friends. I had met him when he came to work as a reserve officer for the sheriff's office that I worked for. I was a field training officer responsible for training new hires and supervising them until they had been trained up to standard to go on duty by themselves.

Russel was a beautiful person and from the beginning we hit it off. Russel was a successful professional commercial deep water diver. He also owned several rental properties and was a accomplished business man. More than that he was just one of the coolest guys I had ever met. I think he was just a few years younger than me and man let me tell you he had a zeal for police work.

At the time I was still in uniform patrol and Russ had to ride with me and go through the rigorous training process. Keep in mind that he was doing all of this in his free time and for free. Reserve deputies are paid nothing. I know that sounds crazy but Russ was truly the kind of guy who wanted to help people as well as he loved to catch bad guys. During his training he was fun to work with and super smart. We had such good times working together that often when I got home in the mornings I felt like I should have had to pay the sheriff for the pleasure of working there.

Russel completed the training and we had even more fun when he came to work on shift with us. He chose to work with our shift so we could work together. I will never forget the fun we had and he quickly became a fine law enforcement professional.

At that time he was married and had no children. Soon his passion for policing overcame him and he was hired on, full time, as a deputy. Not long after that I was promoted to detective but Russ and I still hung out on our free time. We loved all of the same things. Diving and hunting to name a few.

I remember one night being called out to a death scene when I was the detective on call. Russ had been the first one on scene and he called me. He told me the man was on the floor of his bedroom and that he was obviously dead as the blood had drained to the lower part of his body and lividity had set in.

I told him to not let anyone into the scene and rope it off. I once again was going to treat it like a homicide until I could prove otherwise. Now, normally if a body is fresh and we were not there yet I would have had Russ escort in the Acadian Ambulance Paramedics to run a strip on the deceased to see if there was any heart or body activity. In a case where the deceased is on the floor and you can see its obvious they have been there along time (your blood will drain to the lowest point of gravity when your heart stops pumping the blood drains to that point and the skin appears a reddish purple color almost like bruising where all of the blood has pooled inside of the body) but in this case that was not necessary as the man had been dead for a long period of time.

I was on my way to the scene when Russ called and said one of the paramedics was demanding to go in and see the body. I told Russ no not to let him. If it was some type of homicide then defense attorneys love to try to say that any evidence, DNA or otherwise, was carried in by some detective or paramedic, etc.

When I knew a person was deceased, the first thing I had asked was for uniform deputies to rope off a huge area around the home, much more than was needed in case there was some evidence that could be found outside at a later time. I also knew that Russ had been on enough death scenes, that I had taught him well and if he said the guy was dead, then he was dead.

Even on scenes where paramedics are admitted they have to be documented in case we need them at a later date to exclude them as possible sources of DNA or fingerprints that could be found inside the scene. Now we are not talking about a active crime scene where someone is bleeding out, for example, this scene was probably going to be a overdose or heart attack. There was absolutely no reason for anyone to go inside this scene. Being the first responder to the scene Russ' job was to offer any help if he could, (he couldn't because the guy was definitely dead) then to secure the scene and to keep a log book of anyone who entered and what time they entered or exited. That included me or any other detective.

So, I pull up as close to the house as I can and park. I'm still a hundred yards away from the house as the street is blocked with police units and the Acadian ambulance and several volunteer firefighters vehicles. I'm walking towards the house when I observe an Acadian paramedic talking to several volunteer firefighters.

He was very angry and was saying, "I don't know who the hell that deputy thinks he is telling me I can't go into that scene. I will have his badge for stopping me. I am going to write him up and file a formal complaint against him. His ass belongs to me."

I kept walking and met Russ and went into the residence. The deceased was a elderly male probably in his 80's. He was lying face down at the foot of his bed in his underwear and yes lividity was present.

I made contact with the family and they stated that he had serious heart problems and had had many surgeries and heart attacks.

Russ and I waited for the coroner who arrived and talked to the family about his medical history and observed all of the medications he was on. The coroner ruled it as natural death. We had inspected the body and there was no sign of any injuries. The funeral home personnel arrived and were admitted and bagged the body and left.

I was packing up my stuff and talking to Russ when the Acadian paramedic that I had heard bad mouthing Russ outside came in with a pen and clipboard.

He said to Russ, "Deputy, I need your name for my report."

Russ was a easy going guy and he responded and answered the question. The paramedic then asked for Russ badge number. Now when someone asks for your badge number it is usually to harass an officer or to threaten them when they are working. I mean why else would you need a badge number when you can see the name plate the officer is wearing and you know its easy to find out if the officer is lying about his name. So asking for or demanding to know a officer badge number after asking for his name is generally considered a sign of disrespect.

I then interrupted the paramedic and told him we weren't going to play his game. He looked shocked because I didn't say it in a nice way. I told him I knew he was offended that Russ had not let him onto the scene and I further stated that Russ had been following my orders. I then told the paramedic that he could take my name down and I spelled it out for him to make it crystal clear. I then followed, unsolicited, with my badge number. I told him if he was going to write someone up make sure it was me and that he spelled my name correctly. I then told him my scene was still active and he had violated and potentially contaminated it by entering without permission.

I turned to Russ and said, "Get his name and paramedic number and I will have to call his supervisor and explain how the paramedic showed no respect for us as officers on the scene."

The paramedic started stumbling his words and as he was retreating out the door he was apologizing and his skin had turned as white and pale as the deceased gentleman whose house we were in. After he left Russ and I had a good laugh. We never did hear anything else from that paramedic.

I had been on the Special Response Team for the department for some years. Basically it is a more politically correct way of saying SWAT. I guess the powers that be decided that Special Response team sounded more politically correct than Special Weapons and Tactics.

Anyway, back then we would get called out to serve any kind of high risk search or arrest warrant as well as to any kind of scene that had the potential of high violence such as a hostage standoff or manhunt, for example.

Basically the special response team is who the police call when they get scared. Being on the team required true dedication as we didn't get paid, then it was strictly volunteer and the training and call outs were both rigorous and demanding. Not to mention that you had to tryout for the team and it required that you have at least two years in Uniform Patrol, be in top physical shape and have superb marksmanship.

The selection process was lengthy and included in person interviews by team members. Only the best of the best were selected. Russ had actually passed the selection process and had been voted on at the same time I was giving it up.

In addition to all of the volunteer time I gave to SRT, I was carrying my full detective load and it had become a bit overwhelming. As I dedicated myself to detectives, I had less time for my physical training and being called out in the middle of the night was never a quick process. Having to be in my detective office at 8am no matter if you had slept or not began to take it's toll on me.

I talked to Russ about it and he told me that I had made such a positive impact on many of the younger guys careers as well as having paid my dues with SRT and that I should consider what I really wanted to achieve in my career which he knew was to be the go to detective and to be able to solve cases that no one else could.

I took his advice and resigned from SRT. Most SRT officers long weapon of choice was and still is the AR 15 rifle. I was qualified with the weapon and had used it in the Army. But my weapon of choice for high risk entry was my tactical shotgun and I loved that shotgun. I gave the shotgun to Russ so it would be loved and treated the way I did. I know most of you wont understand how sentimental that shotgun was to me but it was my privilege to give it to Russ as there was no one else I would have wanted to have it.

So when the news announcer said that the officer that had died in the fiery crash was Russel Kiger, I cried like a baby. Russ had transferred to the Baton Rouge City Police Department not long after I transferred to the Louisiana State Police.

We kept in contact but not as much as we used to. When we talked it was as if no time had ever passed between us and that is my definition of a true friend. One that you can be away from for long period of time and when you see or talk it is like you never missed a beat.

Russ and I shared that connection. We also had both been through bad divorces and then remarried to awesome wives who were both pregnant with our unborn sons.

I remember being so excited when he told me about their pregnancy, thinking our boys could grow up together the same age and be friends like we were. I also know that Russ was madly in love with his new wife, as I was with mine. We talked about the bad times we had to go through for God to bless us with our soul mates.

Now, in the midst of the pain and the hospital I couldn't get Russ out of my head. I knew I would miss his funeral, I wondered about what he experienced at his dying moment as my time on the emergency room table was still fresh in my mind.

I will state without a doubt that Russ is in heaven as I know he was a Christian. I texted another really good friend of mine that night and asked that if I didn't make it, if he would not only make sure my unborn son would know what kind of man his dad was but that he would make sure that Russ's son knew how awesome of a man, cop, and friend his dad was and that he impacted my life greatly.

I love you Russ, Rest in Peace brother. We will meet again.

So the one time I turned on the television I hear that one of my best friends died in a horrible crash. I didn't turn the television on again while in the hospital.

CHAPTER 21

Two weeks had passed and I was still incapacitated in the hospital. No one was able to tell me what was wrong. Test after test revealed nothing even though I kept demanding it started with the bump on my head. My pain doctors were doing their job. I had so much dope being pumped into me around the clock that all I could do was lay there in the dark. Thank God that I cant remember all of the suffering clearly. Cyndi, however was not medicated and at 5 months pregnant she sat in the dark protecting and praying over me.

On a Saturday, two weeks after I had been admitted by Dr. Surek, he came into my room wearing golf clothes. By that I mean a loud pink polo shirt and plaid shorts. Funny how I can remember that clearly.

Dr. Surek came in just before noon. I had not seen him in two weeks as my case had been handed to neurologist's and he was an Ear Nose Throat specialist. Cyndi and I were both surprised to see him.

Dr. Surek didn't hesitate and stated, "Brother, I have been praying about you and today when I was on the golf course God told me what was wrong with you. God told me just as clear as day what you have. I couldn't wait so I came right away so that you could know."

I remember looking at the doctor and then at Cyndi waiting to hear what he had to say.

Dr. Surek said, "Woody, you have a disease called Trigeminal Neuralgia. It is commonly referred to as "the suicide disease." They call it this because most people that have it end up killing themselves because they cannot live with the pain. Trigeminal Neuralgia is one of the most painful diseases known to man and it is caused by something pressing against the trigeminal nerves which are nerves that are on the side of your head. When something presses against these nerves it is debilitating. Most people only have the pressure on one side of the head and they end up killing themselves from the pain. Woody your case is even more rare because you have it on both side of your head and that is probably why the neurologist haven't thought to diagnose it because it just does not happen. People just don't get it on both sides of their head.

God showed me today when I was on the golf course and I had to come right away to tell you. I know I am not your doctor anymore but when God tells me I obey. I am calling your doctors to confer and tell them what God told me. I will pray for you Woody and pray that God will comfort you and your family."

He then hugged Cyndi and I.

Now Cyndi is a talker and she asked Dr. Surek to step out of the room and answer her questions as the noise from their voices was causing me extreme pain. After some time she came back in and lay with me and held me and we prayed.

Monday came and the neurologist came to examine me again and they all agreed that Dr. Surek was correct and that I had the suicide disease.

My parents came and consulted with the doctors along with Cyndi. I was then told that my life as I knew it was over. The doctors told me that I would be a invalid as there was no cure for the disease and it would never get better. I would be on the pain medications for the rest of my life. No more career. No being normal. The best they could hope for was to try to manage the pain and they said they would start me on nerve drugs to go along with all that I had been prescribed by the pain doctors and basically my life as I had known it was over.

The only thing they could try to help me was to perform surgery and cut the nerves to my face leaving me paralyzed for the rest of my life and that in itself was no guarantee that the pain would stop.

CHAPTER 22

Wow, what news. I couldn't do anything but lay there in pain as I had been but Cyndi and my parents kicked things into high gear. They researched every thing they could find about the disease and confirmed what the doctors had said. It had to be distressing for the people who loved me most to find out how serious my disease was and to ponder my future. They didn't stop though. They contacted the best neurologist's in the country who specialized in Trigeminal Neuralgia. They made appointments with no less than five different neurologist's and while I was in the hospital 3 of those examined me and confirmed what God had told Dr. Surek which was that I was suffering from the suicide disease and my life would never be the same.

A few days later I was finally released from the hospital. I had two more doctors to see who were considered the best in the country on the disease. One was in Boston, Massachusetts and the other was in Lafayette, Louisiana. The doctor in Boston made a appointment to see me in five weeks as that was the earliest opening he had. The doctor in Lafayette couldn't see me for at least 7 weeks. Both had looked at my file and had stated to expect no different diagnosis, basically they gave no real hope that I would be healed.

So I returned home and although I was glad to be out of the hospital it was no real consolation as I was being told the best I could hope for was to be paralyzed. Little did I know that returning home was just the beginning of the hell I was experiencing. When you think things cant get worse trust me, they can.

Cyndi and I returned home and I was so glad to be out of the hospital and thought I would finally at least be able to rest without some hospital worker coming in the room every hour.

What we didn't know was that the different nerve medications the neurologist had put me on the two days before I was discharged would literally make me lose my mind. One was Neurontin and I can't remember the name of the other. When they entered my brain my sanity left. I don't know if it was because of the combination of all the pain medications and the nerve medications but before I started taking the nerve medications I had been suffering and after the nerve medications I went from suffering to a lunatic. I literally entered a mental state of hell.

CHAPTER 23

What I am about to write is just the things I can remember. The rest will be some things that happened that Cyndi told me about later. I had entered Hell on earth.

Upon my arrival home Cyndi and I set in to my daily routine which consisted of me being medicated every three hours with the different pain and nerve medications. I would stay in my bed all day never getting up. At 9pm Cyndi would give me my night medications.

The results of the combination of the pain medications and the nerve medications that occurred were shocking.

I would stay up and watch television and eat some of what ever Cyndi had cooked for me. I never ate much and during those two months of sickness I lost over thirty five pounds. Certainly it was not from exercise as I did absolutely nothing and the farthest I moved in a day would be from my bed to the bathroom. I just didn't eat.

To make matters worse I couldn't have a bowel movement. In fact, I did not have one the whole two weeks plus that I was in the hospital and they were not going to discharge me until I did. I convinced them that I was not in pain from my bowels and to let me go. I don't remember when I was able to go again but it was definitely after I got home. It seems that a side affect of the amount of pain medication I was on was constipation. Honestly that was the least of my problems.

After my 9 pm medications things began to get weird. I am going to tell you of some of the incidents I remember and I thank God that I can't remember more. Cyndi however remembers them all. Even until this day she cannot discuss that time without crying. It seems that the combination of medications made me a very angry person. Cyndi told me that she could set her watch and that after two and a half hours I would start saying how I wasn't going to take the medications anymore and of course she would respond that I had to.

Cyndi then stated that I would become angry and as the next thirty minutes would pass I would become so angry that I would shout and rant and rave that I wasn't going to take the medications anymore no matter what she said. Cyndi stated that it got so bad on a couple of nights she called her brother because she was afraid I was going to get violent. She said she kept him on the phone until the cycle continued where I would go from a angry shouting madman to where I began to feel the pain coming back. When this occurred I went from being adamant that I would never taking the medicines again to being in the fetal position and crying when the pain returned and begging her to give me the medicine.

This behavior was new for me and I had never raised my voice in anger or ever made my wife feel scared for her safety. I know that it was bad because one night she called my parents who live approximately ten miles away when she could not get her brother on the phone. I remember that night. I was in a rage and seeing red. I was convinced that Cyndi was trying to hurt me and I was shouting and cursing her to the point that she locked herself in the bathroom and called my parents. I didn't know she had called them and when they arrived I was shocked because it was in the middle of the night. I still continued to be in a rage as my parents took me to the living room and tried to calm me. I told them that I was convinced Cyndi was killing me with the medications. They sat with me to calm me and as the time passed and my medications began to wear off I again reverted back to practically begging for medication to ease the horrible pain. Cyndi had done nothing wrong and the Woody that was not being pounded by the poison in my veins and brain knew and still does know that she is my angel.

After that night they made me a emergency appointment the next day to see my neurologist. My physical state had sunk to the point where my body would violently shake and I could not complete a sentence. It was bad and getting worse.

CHAPTER 24

Cyndi took me to the doctor and my neurologist wasn't able to see me so one of his partners fit me in. I can remember shaking violently while on the exam table.

The doctor asked me questions and I couldn't speak without stuttering. The doctor observed all of the track marks on my arms and hands that were still healing from the hospital where as I stated earlier every time the nurses would try to start a new IV they would miss the veins. I don't think I had a vein on me that they hadn't tried to tap. The evidence that remained were arms and hands which were in various states of healing from the puncture wounds. If I had stopped myself on the street as a experienced cop and saw all of the track marks and bruising I would have immediately thought that I was dealing with a junkie. Evidently this neurologist thought the same thing.

From what I can remember and what Cyndi has told me the doctor was a rude ass from the time he entered the exam room. It seemed his mood worsened as he saw me laying on the table shaking uncontrollably and observing my track marks and that I was unable to speak.

He told Cyndi that I was a junkie. Yep, just like that he said his problem is that he is a junkie. I guess he wanted to put it in terms that Cyndi could understand. Cyndi tried to explain that it was his partner that had prescribed the nerve medications that interacted with my pain medications and that my shaking and stuttering and violent outburst had not started until after I had returned home from the hospital. She further told the doctor that I had not had any of the symptoms that I now displayed until after they had started the different nerve medications which his partner had prescribed literally as I was getting out of the hospital.

This doctor didn't want to hear it. He stated it was the pain medicine doctors that had got me in this condition.

When Cyndi tried to tell him that I was on the same amount of medicine in the hospital for two weeks and that I had never been like this and that the only change was the nerve medicine that his partner had prescribed the doctor became impatient and angry.

He pointed out the track marks on my arms and hands and said this mans problem is that he is a junkie. The track marks are proof that he is a junkie.

Cyndi was crying and began to get angry with the doctor. She tried to explain how every time the hospital staff tried to start a IV they had to stick me in several places and that they even had to call a nurse from the emergency room to come find a vein. She told him that I had never shot up in my life.

The doctor responded, "You aren't with him all of the time and it's obvious that he shoots up his medications when you are not there. He is a junkie and needs to detox."

This sent Cyndi into a rage. My wife is like my mother when it comes to being a southern belle. They both thrive on proper etiquette and being prim and proper. I am not saying that this is a bad thing and in fact it is one of the things I love the most about Cyndi and my mother. What this doctor didn't know is that when Cyndi gets really mad the southern belle goes out the window. This time was no different.

Cyndi tore into the doctor almost yelling that my condition was not of my own doing and certainly was not something that I was doing to get high. She further told him that I had spent my adult life fighting crime and putting dirt bags in prison. Cyndi was almost shouting and her tears were from anger and I think the doctor was taken aback.

From what I remember this doctor was a big man over 6 feet and probably 250 pounds. When my 5 foot 4 inch pregnant angel lost her southern belle and started in on the doctor he actually took a step back as if he was afraid Cyndi was going to attack him, and to tell the truth she probably was just about at that point.

The doctor said that he was not going to argue, and the only thing he could do for me was surgery. He stated that if I took no medication for 12 hours he would put me on the operating table and cut all of the nerves to my face and paralyze me for life. This was not the first time cutting me and paralyzing me for life had been discussed with a doctor, but it was the first time it had been suggested when Cyndi was seeing red.

Cyndi told him, "So that's it? That's your answer? Take a husband and father and a career law enforcement professional and cripple him for life because you refuse to believe the medicines that your partner prescribed, as almost an after thought, are causing some type of violent reaction. You won't even consider the fact that y'all could be wrong. I have been with him every minute of every day and I can tell you with a certainty that all of the side effects he is having didn't start until after y'all prescribed the nerve medications. It's a damn shame that you are so sure of yourself that you won't consider what I'm telling you and that you are willing to paralyze and cripple him for life."

Cyndi then helped me up and we returned home and the nightmare continued. We had no idea how bad it would get.

CHAPTER 25

We returned home and my condition deteriorated quickly. I began to hallucinate.

The hallucinations seemed to be worse at night time. I will attempt to describe what I can remember. Although I know in my heart that I will never be able to come close to how bad they actually were.

Our house is way out in the country and we have no neighbors and are surrounded by hills and trees. I'm thankful for that as when the hallucinations kicked in I know if I had neighbors they would have called 911 if they had seen me.

The first hallucination I remember was that demons were chasing me. I'm talking about demons that are scarier than anything that you have ever seen on any movie. I remember being in my bed and seeing the demons come out of the walls. They were horribly disfigured beings that looked like they had been burned in the fires of hell. Not only did I see them, I could smell them. They smelled like sulfur and burnt flesh. When I first saw the demons I literally jumped from the bed and took off running. They chased me right out of my house into my yard and they were screaming that they wanted my soul and that they were taking me to Hell. Remember this wasn't a dream. I saw these demons with my own eyes when I was wide awake and I smelled them and heard them and they were just as real as anything I had ever experienced.

I remember laying in my bed and in the dark as seeing light hurt my head. When the first demon came screaming at me I immediately started praying as I was scared to death. Remember that I had learned from Pastor Vicks about how Satan was real and that true evil was real. I immediately started praying out loud, saying the Lord's Prayer. I kept a crucifix beside my bed that was made from a olive tree from Bethlehem and at the base of the crucifix was a glass circle which contained dirt from the earth in Bethlehem. I had purchased this crucifix from missionary workers that had been to Bethlehem about two years before. This crucifix became my sword as I grabbed it I turned on the light hoping that the demon would disappear. No such luck. I held the crucifix in front of me and it stopped the demon inches from my face where I held the crucifix as I prayed. It seemed as if the demon could not get me as long as I was holding the crucifix and praying the Lords Prayer. I was terrified.

While that demon appeared to be stopped by the crucifix and prayer more demons came out of the walls and surrounded me. I tried to pray harder and fight them back. I cannot tell you how many demons there were but it was several and it seemed the longer I stayed in the bed the more monsters surrounded me so I used the oldest defense to man. I ran.

I jumped from the bed with no clothing, as I sleep in the nude. I ran as fast as I could. I tore open my bedroom door without looking back and ran and opened my front door and sprinted out into my front yard. I was stark naked and praying so loud that I was shouting. I started swinging the crucifix and it would make the demons retreat momentarily. I don't know how long I ran around the yard praying and fighting the demons with the crucifix. Remember I was seeing the demons in real life. I was not dreaming and how do I know this? I had a living witness-- Cyndi.

She later told me that she had been asleep when she heard me start to scream and that I turned on the light and grabbed the crucifix and was praying frantically. She said she tried to talk to me to find out what was wrong but that I was oblivious to her and moments later I sprang from the bed in a dead sprint as if Satan himself was chasing me. From what I could see his minions were. She stated that I ran around the yard naked swinging the crucifix and shouting in a terrified voice for the demons to flee and to go back to hell and that I was shouting prayers. She stated that I was crying and swinging the crucifix as if my life depended on it. Of course she couldn't see what I was seeing. She couldn't see the demons or hear their shrieks or smell the stench. All she knew was that the love of her life was running around the house in stark terror and naked as the day he was born.

I don't remember what made the demons go away or how long the episode lasted. Eventually I returned to bed exhausted but I wouldn't sleep and I lay clutching the crucifix and my bible. I also would not turn off the light as I was truly afraid if I did turn it off I would be inviting the demons to attack again.

As the days went by I continued to hallucinate. The hallucinations usually started not long after I took the combination of the pain and nerve pills. When I say nerve pills I don't mean Xanax or some pill to control anxiety I mean Neurotin and the other whose name I cannot recall that were supposed to alleviate pain in my nerves but were non narcotic.

CHAPTER 26

Other hallucinations that I remember vividly were that I was on the witness stand testifying in my old murder cases. I remember seeing the courtroom and jury clearly as if I was there. I would answer the questions of the prosecutor and then when the defense turn came I would answer theirs. I would be so fired up emotionally just as I had been for the real murder trials.

Every murder case I ever worked I took personally and I fought for the victim to have justice. I never lost a murder case that I was a part of. When I built my cases I went above and beyond. These cases went to trial not because the defendant thought he had a chance of a not guilty verdict. They went to trial because they were first degree murder and death penalty cases.

When the District Attorney decided not to go for the death penalty it meant that trial was imminent. You see when the DA took the death penalty off the table then the charge became second degree murder and the minimum a bad guy would get is life without parole, and no defense attorney was going to plead their client to life without parole.

When the death penalty came off the table the defense automatically went to jury trial in hopes that they could get their client a lesser murder offense. Defense attorneys did this even though in many cases I had got full confessions from the dirt bag killers. Like I said though taking the death penalty off the table gave them a free shot at hoping the detectives or the DA would screw up and the charge would come back less.

Usually defendants that the DA would proceed with first degree murder (death penalty) against the murder's would agree to plead to life without parole (second degree murder) in exchange for not having to go to trial and face the death penalty.

The District Attorney had reasons not to pursue the death penalty which could be that the victims family didn't want the bad guy put to death or the most common one was the expense that it cost to put a person to death had to be paid for by the parish. Most people do not know that it cost way more to put a person to death than it does to house him for the rest of their natural life. It cost approximately 15 million dollars for the state to put a person to death due to the length of years and the cost of appeals that are mandatory in any death case. In comparison it would only cost the state approximately one million dollars to house a person in prison until they died and that formula at the time was considering that the average prisoner would live at least forty years after being convicted.

It seemed that I relived the trials of the worst murderers, word for word. Again, I had a witness.

Cyndi stated that I would sit up in bed for hours and answer questions about gruesome murders from attorneys that she couldn't see. She did say that from time to time I would lean over to her and say did you hear that question? Or something to that effect about what ever case I was hallucinating at the time.

Another hallucination that I had numerous times and that I can recall clearly would happen at night. I would be in my bed with Cyndi sleeping and the light in the room on. I would hear birds talking outside and they would call me out to talk to them. I would go outside and hear their distinct call and I would answer repeating the call with my voice. The birds then would respond to my call and I would call back to them. I remember that this fascinated me.

The first night I spent talking to the birds Cyndi awoke and came to sit outside in the darkness with me. I kept asking her could she hear them and she lied and said she could. I didn't know she was lying to me at the time. I think she was just glad that I wasn't running crying and screaming from demon attacks.

I talked to the birds almost every night after that and I really enjoyed it. Cyndi would see that I was okay and return to bed for much needed rest. There is no telling how many hours I spent walking around my yard talking to these birds but it was just as real as anything I had ever experienced.

CHAPTER 27

On the day of my next scheduled appointment for my pain doctor I told Cyndi that I wasn't going. She had gotten up and got ready and then came to wake me. I adamantly refused and said I wasn't going to anymore doctors. I then went back to sleep. Unbeknownst to me Cyndi had called my dad and told him that I was refusing to go. He came to the house and looked into my bedroom and saw me in what appeared to be a seizure. He would later tell me that I was shaking and that my body was jerking and convulsing and that I was talking to someone who wasn't there.

Obviously it was one of many hallucinations that I don't remember. My dad said it scared him and he had never seen anything like it. Needless to say he got me up and made me agree to go to the doctor and stated that he was going to meet us in Baton Rouge at the doctors office.

I vividly remember sitting in the waiting room at the doctors office and that my dad came in and was carrying a magnolia flower and gave it to Cyndi.

At the time I thought that was so strange plus my heightened sense of smell I could really smell the flower. I didn't know it at the time but that apparently was my dads way of telling Cyndi that he was sorry and that they had no idea how bad of shape I was in and ultimately I believe it was a thank you from him to her for taking care of me.

The other thing I remember was that I fell to the floor in the waiting room and was flopping around like a fish. I was bouncing as if having a grand mal seizure. It was crazy and I didn't know why someone wasn't rushing to help me. Turns out, it was another hallucination as when I asked both Cyndi and Dad about it later they stated that I had not ever fallen to the floor but that I was shaking uncontrollably in the chair.

I didn't remember but Cyndi told me afterward that the doctor took me off of the Neurotin when he saw what bad shape I was in. In taking me off the Neurotin he increased my heavy pain medication doses. He upped my levels of Oxycontin and Demerol by a huge amount to compensate and after we left the doctor's office when Cyndi told me we had to stop at another pharmacy I told her that was it. When she asked me what was it, I told her that we had to go back to Dr. Surek and that I had to convince him to take the knot off the back of my head. Cyndi agreed as she knew none of the pain had started until that Monday after Easter when I felt the knot come up on the back of my head.

We drove straight to Dr. Surek's office and even though he wasn't my doctor anymore and hadn't been for some time he made time to see me. Even though his waiting room was packed he cared enough when Cyndi told his nurse all that was going on he ushered us into his private office.

I then told him I had to have the knot removed from my head . He stated there was no way I could have this surgery because it was a major surgery even though it was a small knot and that I was in such bad condition already. I told Dr. Surek that I had five weeks until I let a neurosurgeon cut all the nerves to my face and cripple me for life. I literally begged him to do the surgery as I knew that that knot that all of the doctors had said was nothing but a fatty lipoma was the root of the evil I was going though. Dr. Surek told me that little knot would not cause trigeminal neuralgia as the nerves that were causing the pain were on the top sides of my head and that knot was no where near the nerves. I was holding Cyndi's hand and we begged him to do the surgery.

He was quiet for a few minutes as he intently stared at me from his chair.

Then he shook his head in the affirmative and said " Okay, be at the hospital at 5 am to check in and I will do the surgery at 7 am."

He followed that with the warning that it was still a major surgery and that I would have to be in the hospital for about a week and that I would have a drain in my head and stitches. I stated that I didn't care and that I just wanted the knot gone. He agreed and we left.

CHAPTER 28

The next morning around 4 am Cyndi drove me to the hospital. We checked in and my parents arrived. Before the staff took me back I was prepped and Dr. Surek came in and explained the surgery in detail. He stated that they would shave the small area over the knot and make a small incision and then he would remove the lipoma and that the surgery should just take a few minutes. After the surgery I would be taken to ICU for observation and in a few hours I would be moved to my room.

While he was talking to us the anesthesiologist came in and said that they would put me under using general anesthesia and he would be the one in charge. For some reason I asked if there was a way they could do the surgery without putting me to sleep. To tell the truth I was afraid of the darkness and what I might experience. I know that I shouldn't have been. I knew if I died Jesus would come for me as he had that night in the emergency room. I was afraid of what I would experience while being forced to sleep. The Demons that had chased me were still very fresh in my mind and still scared me. I had not slept with the lights off since that had happened. In fact I slept with my crucifix and bible and placed other crucifix's around my bed every time I went to sleep.

Cyndi has always had a love of crosses and in our home we had a wall that was decorated with numerous crosses that she had acquired over the years. After that first time fighting demons I had taken all of the crosses and placed them around my bed in a circle. It was my attempt to keep the demons away and another show of how much Cyndi loved me as anyone else would have had me committed.

I asked the doctors again if I had to be put to sleep and Dr. Surek said, "No, you don't. We can do it while you are awake, although that is highly unusual."

The anesthesiologist agreed and stated that he could numb my head and that I could stay awake although he didn't recommend it because I would fill the tugging on my head.

I said that I just didn't want to be put to sleep and I didn't care about them tugging or what ever they had to do and that Dr. Surek said it would just be a small incision. The doctors agreed.

They then left us alone stating that we would have a few minutes before they came to wheel me into surgery. Cyndi and my dad and mom and I prayed, and prayed, and prayed. I told them how much I loved them and they each told me how much they loved me and that everything was going to be fine. Soon the nursing staff came and wheeled me out the room and my family followed down the hall as far as the staff would let them go. After one more round of hugs and kisses I was wheeled through double doors and down a corridor and into a brightly lit surgery room. I was moved to the surgery table and placed face down on the table and it had a doughnut shaped hole that my face went into so that I was immobilized and looking at the floor. I remember the anesthesiologist talking to me as he numbed me. Then Dr. Surek talked to me and I don't remember many details of the surgery I just remember people talking and I remember the staff adjusting my head and body at different times. I do remember that the surgery seemed to take forever and that I was awake.

The next memory I had was awakening in the ICU recovery room. I was in a mobile bed and there were beds on either side of me with a nurses station in front of me. I wasn't the only one recovering from surgery, and the nurses kept checking me.

Dr. Surek came in and he was smiling. In fact he appeared to be very happy. He checked the drain on the back of my head and then stood above me and I swear its almost as if he was beaming with this huge grin on his face. I tried to talk to him but he told me to rest. He told me that the surgery had gone unbelievably well and that in a few hours I would be moved to my room. He told me he had already talked to Cyndi and my parents and that they would be in the room when I got there.

The whole time he was talking to me he kept smiling and I thought, *Man there is one happy guy. He must really love doing surgery if it makes him smile this much.*

Some hours had passed and I had fallen asleep. I was awoken by nurses as usual every few minutes, it seemed, for medication and for them to check the drain in my head. Finally I was wheeled through the hallways and up a elevator and into the room where my family was waiting.

When I was rolled into the room I saw Cyndi and my dad and mom and they all were smiling and seemed to be in a joyous mood. I was moved to my bed and was in real bad pain from the surgery but everyone around me was smiling like they were at a party or something. Once I was in the bed, Cyndi got on one side of me holding my hand and my parents were on the other side. Finally, I asked why was everyone smiling. I told them Dr. Surek had been smiling from ear to ear. They were all beaming and I was curious.

Cyndi asked me if Dr. Surek had told me anything.

I asked, "Told me what?" I stated that he told me the surgery went really well and that's all he said.

My mother couldn't contain herself and she said, "Baby, when Dr. Surek cut you open to take out that little knot he said it was bigger than he thought so he kept making your incision longer and longer. It turned out that you had a tumor that covered the entire back side of your head and the base of your skull. The tumor was unusual as it appeared to grow upwards."

Dr. Surek said that it was the biggest tumor he had ever seen and that it took him a long time to scrape it from my skull and to cut it away from my spine.

In the end the small tumor that all of the neurosurgeons and other doctors and MRI and CT-scans had said was nothing and could not cause me pain ended up being the size of a soft ball. A huge tumor that was non cancerous. Dr. Surek further stated that he had never seen this type of tumor return after it was removed. To sum it up Dr. Surek was astonished by what he found when he cut me open.

As a result of the long incision he made to get to all of the tumor my drain in my head was enormous and was closed with over thirty staples. My scar is to this day approximately eight inches long. That's a far cry from the small one half inch incision that was planned. I knew as my mother was telling me what the doctor had said as I looked at Cyndi crying tears of joy and my father was smiling from ear to ear. He looked like he wanted to dance a jig. I knew then as I know now that I am truly loved.

CHAPTER 29

I was in the hospital for almost a week due to the seriousness of the surgery and the size of the open wound on my head. It definitely was not fun and I was in severe pain although thankfully I don't remember much of it due to the heavy narcotics. Cyndi never left my side and watched over me like a mother hen. Dr. Surek saw me every day to check the drain and supervise the changing of my head bandages which made me look like a mummy. The week passed and I was finally discharged and sent home to recover. I had to go to Dr. Surek's office every three days for him to change bandages and inspect the wounds recovery.

I was still on all of my medicines that I had been on before the surgery but in that first week home I noticed a difference. I had severe pain from the surgery but I no longer had the blinding, crippling pain that I had suffered from since that Monday night after Easter. I didn't tell anyone at first until I was sure, and then I only told Cyndi that I wanted to get off of the medications. She at first thought I was being like before the surgery and was going to argue that I did not need the medications because I hated the way they made me feel. I then told her that I had no more pain like I did before the surgery and that while I still needed pain medication to help me endure the recovery but the old pain was gone.

We agreed not to tell anyone and to see how it went as I still had three weeks before I was going to Boston to see the best neurologist in the country and to let him cut all of the nerves and paralyze me. We agreed to not tell my parents or anyone else in case the pain returned as to not get their hopes up.

CHAPTER 30

During this time other people in my life were preparing for me to be disabled for the rest of my days. My father was filling out the paperwork that would officially have me declared as disabled. That's what the doctors had told him to do. Meanwhile he had already filled out all of the federal paperwork for my job with the Louisiana State Police which included the Federal Emergency Medical Leave Act which secured my job for the time being although no one expected me to ever return to duty.

Louisiana State Police Criminal Investigator, Murray Landry, was my closest friend at the State Police. He had served 23 years as a trooper and then retired and was hired back some time later as a Criminal Investigator. Murray was hired two months before the State Police made me the offer for the same position which I accepted on November 1, 2007. We became fast friends as Murray was a avid hunter like me and we were both assigned to the Louisiana State Police Internal Affairs division. More importantly Murray was and is a strong warrior for God. He truly believed in the daily battle that Satan fights for our souls. We shared our experiences both of our love for Jesus and our old school law enforcement mentality.

Murray Landry was around 53 years old when I met him. He is a true coon-ass from Assumption parish where his father was the Sheriff for over 20 years. Murray was no saint growing up and like me he was known more for chasing women and fighting than anything else. In fact, anytime I ever met a older person from Assumption and asked if they knew Murray Landry they all did as he was a legend.

Murray was anything but a average 50 year old. He is approximately 5 foot 10 and weighed maybe 185 pounds of solid muscle. This guy was ripped and had biceps bigger than any other trooper I ever saw. He worked out every day lifting weights, doing pushups and crunches. He would end his workouts by putting on a army ruck sack which he filled with 60 pounds of weight and went and ran numerous miles. He was and still is a beast. In my prime years of my early twenties I would not have fought him at age 53. He is a bad dude.

On the other hand, Murray is as fine as a person that you will ever meet. He is honest and straightforward and extremely intelligent. At the time I met him he had been married over 20 years and had two beautiful daughters. Our offices were connected and we handled business when it came up. We also enjoyed each others company immensely.

While I was at home recuperating my supervisors sent Murray to my house to pick up my unmarked unit to return it to headquarters for storage. What I didn't know was that they had also charged Murray with finding my replacement as they had been told by doctors that I would never work again. Murray of course didn't tell me and that day he came to my home I had taken my first shower since the surgery and I was awake in my recliner when he and Trooper J.B. Slaton came to get my car. He hugged me and said that I looked much better than he had expected. He said he expected to find me in bed knocked out.

Murray has a gift of being able to read people. He can size a person up in a instant and I think he knew that day that I was going to return, that something had changed. I didn't tell him about not having anymore pain except from recovering from surgery but I felt that he knew. I should also mention that the bible I slept with every night was given to me by Murray years before at the office when we were looking up a particular verse. He told me to keep it and I don't know if I ever got to tell him how much it comforted me and protected me during those dark hours of my sickness.

When he left that day I realized he was the first contact other than family and doctors that I had had since I had gotten sick. His visit although on a official basis lifted my spirits. I will always remember our years together and know that I am a better person for having known him. That day when he visited I knew for the first time that I would be healed and that I would return to work.

CHAPTER 31

Cyndi and I started to wean me off the heavy medications. It was not a easy process. I hated the way the pain medications made me feel, but before the surgery I had to have them to take the edge off the pain so that I didn't kill myself to escape it. That being said I was on some serious high doses and I would soon learn that getting off those medicines would be its own type of pain.

I went through full blown withdrawals. I quit taking the Demoral and Oxycontin the day that Murray came to my house. I got very sick during the withdrawals and even puked. I felt as if I had a high fever and I would get the chills and shake uncontrollably. This lasted for maybe 3 or 4 days. Cyndi never left me and saw me through it, cleaning up my puke and holding me during that terrible withdrawal period.

As bad as the withdraws were they were nothing compared to the hell I had experienced before the surgery. I was very sick but I knew it was only temporary as Cyndi had researched what I would experience during the withdrawal and none of it compared to the sickness and pain and hallucinations before the surgery. So it was bad but compared to before the surgery it was a cake walk.

During the withdraw from the Oxycontin and Demoral I still had other pain pills, Lortab and Percocet which help ease the withdraw and control the remaining pain from the surgery. Once I knew I was clean from the Oxycontin and Demoral I began to wean off the Lortab and Percocet. With in two weeks I was off all but ibuprofen.

My doctors visits to Dr. Surek had been cut down to once a week. I had one more week until he was scheduled to remove my staples. I went on the scheduled day and Dr. Surek told me how good I looked. He was very shocked at the difference in my appearance. He then began to remove the staples from my head and that hurt like heck but was nothing compared to what I had experienced before it. He then removed my drain and said he wanted to see me again the next week. Dr. Surek knew that was the week before I was scheduled to go to Boston.

When I returned the following week to Dr. Surek he removed the stitches and told me that he wouldn't need to see me again unless I needed him. He said keep the wound clean and I would make a full recovery. Cyndi and I then told him the news that since he had cut the tumor from me that I had no more pain from the Trigeminal Neuralgia. I told Dr. Surek that he was a true gift from God and that as long as I lived I would owe him my life as if he had not agreed to do the surgery then I would have let them paralyze me. We told him that we loved him and that we would never forget him. There wasn't a dry eye in the room.

Dr. Surek stated that it was God that had led him to diagnose me that day when he was playing golf and that it was God that told him to do the surgery even though his human doctor side said not to. Dr. Surek further stated that he was just a ordinary man who loved Jesus and that Jesus had blessed him with the gift to help heal people and that when he performed surgery his hands were just Gods instruments and that he was thankful and felt truly blessed in helping me heal. We will never forget him.

CHAPTER 32

Cyndi and I drove to my parents house and they were surprised to see us. They had visited some since I had been home from the hospital but never stayed long as they thought I was as bad as I had been. Some of those visits I was going through withdrawals and mostly when they came they brought groceries or meals that my mom had cooked. So they were indeed surprised to see us in their house.

I told them to sit down and that we needed to talk. They did and looked at me half scared of what I was going to say. I told them that I was healed. They were shocked and didn't seem to comprehend. I think my dad might have thought this was me trying to get out of going to Boston. Then I explained in detail what had happened since the surgery and how I detoxed and how we wanted to make sure the Trigeminal Neuralgia was gone before we told them as not to give false hope. In short, I told them that I was completely healed other the wound from my surgery. There was much praising of God for the miracle of the healing.

I know my parents suffered deeply during my sickness. They never let up on praying and hoping for my recovery. My mother had Rosaries said in my name at the Catholic Church and masses where they prayed for me.

My father took over protecting me and from day one I never worried about bills or finances. He also spent hours and days preparing my forms for the Louisiana State Police and for disability. He also kept my supervisor at the state police advised daily on my condition. There is no telling what else he did to sacrifice or fight for me as he is not the type of person to boast or seek approval of others. Like I said before when the chips are down he shines. If I was in war there would be no one I would rather have in my foxhole than him.

Now it was over. I had a new respect for and lease on life. In the next few weeks I returned to the Louisiana State Police and resumed my regular schedule. Each day seemed as it was Christmas. To even be up and moving without medication was crazy compared to where I had been 5 weeks before.

I remember going fishing with my father and we were catching them nonstop and it hit me. Just a few weeks before all doctors had told me that I was going to be a invalid. That I would never have a normal life or work again much less be sitting in a boat catching a ton of fish. Once again I praised God for delivering me.

CHAPTER 33

Finally, I want to write why I think Jesus let me go through this experience. Every year on Good Friday when I would see the stations of the cross I would think of how much Jesus suffered and was tortured before they finally nailed him to the cross and he died.

I would get very mad. Especially when I think that he had disciples who could have fought for him. I used to say that had I been there I would have fought for Jesus and they would have had to kill me before I watched him beaten and tortured and nailed to the cross.

This goes back to my childhood where in the Catholic Church I was raised in had wood replicas hanging along the inside church wall that showed each station of the cross. These were up 365 day a year. Every time I saw them it upset me. I just couldn't fathom that no one would help Jesus.

We know that one man came out and carried the cross for a short distance to help Jesus as he kept falling in the street under the weight of the cross. He was the only one.

Every Good Friday I told myself had I been there I would have done something, and that I was tough enough to take some of the pain for Jesus.

I do not think it is a coincidence that I got sick 3 days after being angry again at seeing the stations of the cross being acted out around the world on the news on that Good Friday. Big bad me. So ready to boast that I would have taken some of the pain for Jesus and that they would have had to kill me before I would let him be treated like that. Well, Jesus humbled me. He showed me that I couldn't have handled it and it didn't take whips and clubs and being nailed to a cross to break me. All it took was a little bump on the back of my head, which left me not only incapacitated but broken and nearly destroyed.

Thank you Jesus for dying on the cross for me, and I know now that I couldn't have done anything and that what you went through was for my benefit. You endured and suffered through it so that I may have a chance to live forever in heaven with you and I praise your holy name.

CHAPTER 34

One final thought- Jesus would have taken that beating,, torture, pain and humiliation to save one soul. If there was only one other person on earth he would have done the same thing and suffered the same way just for one of us. That's how strong his love is. Remember he could have stopped the pain at anytime he could have ended it with one word to God. He chose instead to bear it so that all of his children could go to heaven if they believe in him and ask for forgiveness for their sins. That is powerful.

Afterword

I could have written in much more detail about the specifics of amounts of medicines and doctors and nurse names and appointment times etc. I chose not to and to focus on just a few areas that stood out most in my mind. Ultimately, I wanted to convey the love I felt when Jesus held me and the pain I felt throughout the sickness, and the ultimate joy and victory in my recovery which medical professionals had said would never happen.

I also want to thank everyone for all prayers and other things that were done on my behalf to help during that time. There is no way I can personally thank everyone since I can't remember all of the details of what people did or sacrificed for me. The most I can do is to pray for others especially when I know there is a specific need and give hope to people by sharing my story and telling how Jesus Held Me. Amen.

Made in the USA
Columbia, SC
04 May 2021

36815248R00035